BREAKING
THE STIGMA

BREAKING THE STIGMA

Racism, the Opioid Endemic, Lies, and Inviting Grandma to the Dispensary

Business Strategies for Cannabis Retailers to WIN in the Marketplace

CHARLENA BERRY

ZEPPLYN
PUBLISHING

BREAKING THE STIGMA

Racism, the Opioid Endemic, Lies, and Inviting Grandma to the Dispensary

ISBN 978-1-5445-2892-2 *Hardcover*

      978-1-5445-2893-9 *Paperback*

      978-1-5445-2894-6 *Ebook*

      978-1-5445-2891-5 *Audiobook*

For Joe.

I love you. I love you. I love you.

You're in all the oceans now.

Contents

Foreword

—Anna Shreeve, founder of the Bakeréé

Ten years ago, my son asked me to help him open a medical cannabis business. At the time, the cannabis industry was a gray market, so I was initially hesitant about the idea. I had never used cannabis and had very little knowledge of the plant beyond the stigma I'd been sold about it. My son was incredibly persuasive, though. He revealed to me that he was a cannabis user, which I'd never known, and he explained how much it helped him manage his anxiety. Then he told me, "Mom, there's a lot of people using this product to battle cancer. Maybe someday we could be a part of curing cancer." How could I say no to that? My son had never been so passionate about something before, and I would do literally anything to help my children find their path in life. So I jumped in with both feet, knowing nothing.

Today, our medical dispensary has grown into the Bakeréé, which has two locations in the Seattle area, serving both medical and recreational customers. We've won multiple High Times Cannabis Cups and worked with the University of Washington and the Seattle Cancer Care Alliance in palliative care.

My thoughts and view of cannabis have changed enormously over the years, and my passion for this work has grown to match my son's. That's why I was so excited when I learned Charlena was writing a book. The cannabis industry is still new and developing, and we're at a fork in the road. As retailers, we have two paths we can follow. One is the path of greed, in which we are willing to sacrifice our employees' well-being and even our customers' best interests in the name of profit. Ironically, though, when you prioritize profit over everything else, you damage your customer experience, which ultimately leads to reduced revenue in the long term. This path thus leads to both harm and mediocrity.

The other path is the Charlena Berry path, in which the goal is to be the best retailers we can be, combining retail best practices with a passion for cannabis and for helping people. On this path, we prioritize creating an excellent customer experience that empowers our customers to make the best choices for themselves. We step up as leaders and work to elevate everyone in our industry, at all levels, particularly marginalized individuals who have been most negatively impacted by the war on drugs and the stigma of cannabis. This path leads to sustainable success and growth while doing good for our workers, our industry, and our society.

Like many people in the cannabis industry, I didn't come from a retail background. I worked in media, both radio and television, for over thirty years, first as a salesperson, then director of sales, and finally as a general manager of a CBS-owned and operated television property. Especially in television, everything was constantly changing and progressing—not too different from the cannabis industry today, in which nothing is ever static, with new legislation, evolving customer trends, and advances in the science of cannabis. Being a Hispanic woman in this largely male- and white-dominated space added additional challenges to an already high-pressure job managing many people and being responsible for more than a hundred million dollars in revenue. Many times I felt like the token brown person or the token woman in the room. I felt I had to work harder and do more to prove myself.

Being in that environment taught me a lot of resiliency and adaptability, which have been invaluable to me in the cannabis industry, but what it didn't teach me was how to run a retail store. I've learned many lessons through trial-and-error and hard-won experience, but I wish I instead had Charlena's book when I opened my first store. Charlena has distilled her many years of retail experience and knowledge into practical strategies and tips for success. What makes her book really special, beyond the incredible and valuable advice she offers, is the *inspiration* she offers. I've known and worked with Charlena for three years, and I've found that she respects all people equally and has a special talent for connecting people and elevating businesses in a way that lifts everyone up together. She has a powerful vision for our industry, and with enough Charlena Berrys, I truly believe we can change not just the cannabis industry, but our world.

There's a perception in this industry that if you have enough money, you can succeed. To an extent, that may be true, but to really compete in the long term, you also need true, authentic passion. This passion is often found in people who come from marginalized backgrounds—those who have long recognized the benefits of cannabis and who have been ostracized for utilizing this plant-based medicine for their wellness. In my opinion, these people are creative geniuses. They recognized the truth about cannabis and fought for it despite the stigma and everybody telling them they were wrong.

We need people like this in the industry. They believe in cannabis on a very deep level. They have a love for the plant and a drive to create the highest-quality, safest products for the best price. Because of the historical context surrounding the stigma of cannabis, you'll find that these individuals are often people of color. Unfortunately, due to systemic racism, these people tend to have a more challenging time raising the money needed to start a cannabis business. It's so important for us to invest in and elevate these individuals, because they bring things to our industry that money can't buy: purpose, resiliency, and passion.

Incredible things happen when people with money partner with people who have a passion for the plant. At Bakeréé, we are committed to elevating multigenerational users of cannabis, and the majority of our workers are people of color. We have virtually no turnover and have several employees who have been with us for six to ten years. These people are connected to the plant and understand cannabis on a deep level, and I know they are a huge part of why customers love us and how we've won multiple High Times Cannabis Cups. Most rewarding for me is the opportunity to provide a quicker path to success for people who perhaps feel the way I did working in broadcast management—that because of their race or their background, they have to work harder and do more to achieve success.

This blend of money and passion is Charlena's vision for our industry as well. While you may not know it from looking at her, she comes from a marginalized background herself. In this book, she gives you a look inside not just her brain, but her soul, and I think you will see bits and pieces of yourself in her story. We have thousands of choices every single day, but if we only see the future through our past, we won't recognize all the opportunities available to us. So if you've ever felt like you're not good enough because of your circumstances or background, I hope seeing Charlena's success and passion will inspire you and give you the confidence you need.

There is so much potential in the cannabis industry. We have the opportunity for huge financial rewards as retailers, but we need to do things the right way. Greed is often the default for businesses, but I don't want that. Charlena doesn't want that. And I don't think the cannabis plant wants that either. The plant doesn't want us to cause harm. It was meant to heal, which I learned from personal experience, because three years after my son and I opened our medical dispensary, my husband got cancer. It was stage IV and had spread to multiple locations: his throat, thyroid, and lungs. He had three surgeries and had a lung removed, but there was still cancer in his body, including a spot on his remaining lung. He was pre-signed up for a clinical trial, and that's when we convinced him to go fully vegan and begin daily dosing of a full-spectrum CBD oil. Within a few months, the spot on his lung went away. His oncologist literally said, "He's our miracle for the year." He's been cancer-free for six years now. So I guess my son was right: maybe we were a part of helping cure cancer, for one person at least.

This plant can better people's lives, and that's what we need to do too. We can be an industry that uses and takes advantage of people, or we can be an industry that improves our customers' and employees' lives and betters the world. In picking up this book, you've already taken your first step to creating a better store and a better industry. Cannabis never should've been stigmatized in the first place, so let's work together, become leaders, and break the stigma.

Introduction

Securing a cannabis license is like winning the lottery. After years of persistence, mountains of paperwork, and countless challenges, you're finally able to open your store, and the money pours in. You think all your hard work has paid off, and you can finally relax and reap the rewards.

Everything is great…for a couple of years. Then more stores open in your area. All of a sudden, you have competition. With more choice, your customers begin spending their money elsewhere. At first, you might not realize you have a problem. *Just a slow week,* you think. Then a slow week turns into a slow month, and a slow month turns into a slow year. Your revenue stagnates and may even begin to decline. You slowly fall further and further behind your competitors. You know something needs to change, but you have no idea where to start. You feel completely lost, frustrated, and overwhelmed.

I've seen this same story play out again and again. Because our industry is so new, it can be easy for cannabis retailers to be tricked into complacency. In the early years after a state legalizes cannabis, either medically or recreationally, the product practically sells itself. Supply is limited, and demand is high. You don't have to be an exceptional retailer to make money; you simply need product on the shelves. Many retailers thus experience *accidental success*, and are profitable not because of their actions or business strategy, but simply because of the nature of the market.

Looking forward five, ten, fifteen years, the cannabis landscape will be very different. More states will have legalized medical and recreational use, existing markets will have matured, and cannabis may even be legalized on a federal level. We are not far from a future in which we have as many cannabis stores as we do liquor or grocery stores. As soon as more retailers enter the space, you will no longer be able to rely on accidental success. Simply existing will not be enough to compete. You will need to create a *better customer experience.*

The customer experience can always be improved, and every store, no matter how successful, can benefit from being more intentional about their customer experience. However, if any of the following statements apply to you, improving your customer experience might be more than beneficial; it might be *necessary* to your business's survival:

- Your revenue is stagnating or declining.
- You're getting poor customer reviews online.
- You're struggling to compete with other stores in your area.
- You attract only a narrow type of customer—for example, men in their twenties.
- You have difficulty retaining customers.
- You've never thought about or taken conscious action to improve your customer experience.
- You're in the process of scaling.
- You opened your store without having prior retail experience.

Wherever you are in your journey as a retailer and whatever specific problems you're facing, the long-term health of your business depends on your customer experience. Creating a better customer experience always starts with understanding your customer, and in our market, understanding the customer means understanding the stigma of cannabis.

WHY WE NEED TO BREAK THE STIGMA OF CANNABIS

Although public support of cannabis is increasing, the simple fact is that a stigma remains. For decades, we've been told as a society that cannabis is dangerous, that it turns people into lazy stoners and dirty hippies and leads to harder drugs. That kind of deeply ingrained programming is difficult to undo, and it has led to a fear of cannabis. Parents worry their kids will be corrupted, politicians fear the cannabis industry will attract criminals and other "trash" to their community, and cannabis users are afraid of being judged or punished for their usage.

You and I know that cannabis is safe for most people in most circumstances, and we also know that the cannabis industry has many positive economic, medical, and societal benefits. We must recognize, though, that many of our customers struggle with fear and shame due to the stigma. I've worked in the cannabis industry for years, and even *I* occasionally feel this fear and shame. When I first left the Fortune 500 corporate world, I was embarrassed to tell my former colleagues what I was doing, afraid they would look down on me. Sometimes still today, I get nervous walking into a dispensary, even though I know I shouldn't. I coach my daughter on what to tell people I do for work, because I know that some people won't react well. If you, too, have ever felt nervous or like you had to hide your career in certain situations, then you've experienced the stigma firsthand—and we're professionals! Imagine what it's like for your customers, especially novice or first-time users.

The stigma of cannabis is one of the biggest barriers we face as retailers. It's at least partly why cannabis is still federally illegal and listed as a Schedule I drug, which has created incredible logistical challenges for us. It's why some communities are unwelcoming to dispensaries. It's why many people are too afraid to use cannabis, even if they'd benefit from it. It's why cannabis users are judged as lazy or even criminals and discriminated against through the use of employer drug tests.

As retailers, we are the face of the cannabis industry. We are the ones with the power to change how people think and feel about cannabis. It will be an uphill battle. Because of the existing prejudices, stereotypes, and biases, our bar is set higher than it is in other industries. To break the stigma, we can't just be good retailers; we have to be *great*. We have to work harder, be better, and hold ourselves to a higher standard. It might not be fair, but it's the reality, and it's our responsibility as industry professionals.

I won't pretend like it's easy, but the rewards are worth it. In breaking the stigma, we can broaden our customer base and connect with our customers in a way that inspires loyalty. We can also hopefully encourage better, more just legislation of cannabis, which will make our jobs easier and protect our customers from discrimination. Bottom line: breaking the stigma is good for business, and it's just the right thing to do.

THE CUSTOMER EXPERIENCE IS KEY

The way we break the stigma is through the customer experience. The retail experience we create must overcome the stereotypes. If we can create a delightful experience—one that dispels customers' fears and makes them feel comfortable—we will not only increase customer loyalty and revenue, but we will establish cannabis as a legitimate industry. My goal with this book is to help you create the kind of customer experience that will defy the stigma—a place so welcoming and inclusive that even your grandma would feel comfortable shopping there.

One of the things I love best about the cannabis industry is that it is filled with entrepreneurs and small business owners. These people tend to have a lot of passion and hustle, but they don't necessarily come in with a background in retail, which can put them at a disadvantage. You can know everything there is to know about cannabis, but if you don't also understand fundamental retail principles, your store will struggle. You will unconsciously do things that make some customers feel excluded or that create a poor customer experience.

That's where I come in. I have a master's in supply chain management from Michigan State University, and more than twelve years of experience working for Fortune 500 companies in the retail space, including Whirlpool and Office Depot. During that time, I served in leadership roles, helped navigate major mergers (Whirlpool/Maytag and Office Depot/OfficeMax), and oversaw initiatives related to inventory, process improvement, systems enhancement, and omnichannel functions. I left the corporate world to found Cannabis Business Growth, a cannabis consulting company, where I currently serve as CEO. I have since consulted on more than three hundred cannabis projects across the United States, Canada, Puerto Rico, Africa, and Australia, providing expertise and assistance in compliance, licensing, and business strategy. I've now been working exclusively in the cannabis industry for more than five years.

Basically, what all that means is I understand retail, and I've learned how to translate traditional retail practices to the cannabis industry. The cannabis industry is so new that we don't have much collective knowledge to draw on yet, but the traditional retail industry has been refining best practices for decades. In this book, I share those lessons so that you can become a more effective retailer, which will help you break the stigma and create intentional, instead of accidental, success.

WHY I WROTE THIS BOOK

I have a confession I want to get out of the way early: I do not smoke, vape, or consume cannabis. Aside from the occasional THC bath bomb, I don't use cannabis in any way. Why, as a nonuser, have I chosen to dedicate my time and energy to cannabis and even write a book about it? It's because of my brother Joe.

Joe's story starts innocuously enough, with a headache during a bowling trip with our stepdad, John.[1] The only pain medication John had with him was what he had been prescribed as a cancer patient: OxyContin. This was around 2000, before we knew all we do now about OxyContin. John was told it was safe and nonaddictive. He'd been sent home with a giant 120-pill bottle, as if it were ibuprofen or any other over-the-counter pain medication. So when Joe said his head hurt, John broke an OxyContin in half and handed it to him. His child was in pain, and he did what many parents would do: he gave Joe a medicine he thought was safe and that was readily available, in an excess supply, in our home.

Joe was only fourteen years old. Neither he nor my stepdad knew it at the time, but that tiny half pill would trigger a twenty-year struggle with

---

[1] Throughout the book, some names and identifying details have been changed to protect the privacy of the people involved.

addiction for my brother. As an adult and parent of a thirteen-year-old daughter, I'm mortified that this is how his addiction began. Given the knowledge of opioids at the time, though, and the lies that were presented to doctors by Purdue Pharma (the makers of OxyContin) and the FDA, my stepdad couldn't have known how bad that simple act was. He was just trying to make his kid's headache go away. As parents, all of us must make decisions regarding what medicine to provide our children, with the information available to us.

It wasn't just my brother who got addicted. There were enough Oxys in the house to addict multiple family members and loved ones around John. Before cancer, before opioids, John was a stand-up guy. The opioids turned him into a pretty crappy person who made what I thought were really terrible parenting decisions. In part due to this, I ultimately moved out and sought emancipation at fifteen years old. After I left, my brothers told me dozens of horror stories about his behavior. The opioids weren't solely to blame, but they certainly amplified his negative traits and made living with him miserable. John eventually beat cancer, but he never beat his addiction. He died of an opioid overdose, just a few years after his cancer went into remission.

I often wonder how things would have been different if it weren't for those pills. What if medical cannabis was socially acceptable and legal back then? What if there wasn't a stigma against cannabis, creating shame and fear? What if my stepdad had been offered medical cannabis instead of Oxys to manage his pain during his cancer treatment? Maybe my brother wouldn't have had twenty years of his life stolen from him. Maybe my stepdad and hundreds of thousands like him would still be alive. In my heart, I *know* the trajectories of their lives would have been drastically different, if only John had been given cannabis instead of opioids. I don't ever want someone else to suffer the way my family has, and that's why I'm so passionate about cannabis.

THE UGLY REALITY OF
THE STIGMA AGAINST CANNABIS

Unfortunately, the what-ifs don't matter. The reality is that because of the stigma of cannabis, my stepdad was never offered medical cannabis, and my brother's life was changed, completely and for the worse.

At fourteen, Joe was arrested for selling Oxy at school. While this sounds horrid and it is easy to start the cycle of shaming the addict, let me give you some context. Growing up, we didn't have enough money for basics, like lunch money. Later in life, Joe told me how hungry he was all the time. So with hundreds of Oxys in the house, I can hear the voice in his head: *Who will know if a few go missing? What's the harm?* The doctor would just give John more. The spigot of Oxys was never-ending. Remember also that Joe was a *child*. He didn't understand what he was doing. He had been given his first Oxy by a trusted source, his stepdad, who had gotten his Oxys from a trusted source as well, a doctor. To Joe, it was just medicine, and selling it was a way to fill his belly.

At eighteen, he came to me for the first time with shame, telling me he wanted to clean up his life and have a new beginning. I was twenty-two at the time and living in Michigan, and he was in Florida. For him to have any chance of getting clean, he needed to be in a place where drugs were not as accessible, so I bought him an airline ticket to Michigan. I helped him get a job and let him live with me. Still being rather naive, I didn't know a ton about recovery. I didn't know enough to push him to attend meetings or get a sponsor. I just gave him a chance with a change of scenery. I thought I would put him under my wing, and he would be okay. I couldn't have predicted what would come next.

About three weeks into him living with me, I got a call around 6:20 in the morning. It was our grandmother. "He's gone. He's gone, Char," she told me. Our dad had passed away. It was a huge blow to both me and Joe. One of the worst things I've ever had to do in my life was look him in the eyes and tell him Dad was gone. We sat in silence together for days trying to figure out how to put one foot in front of the other. Together we called our other brother and were responsible for telling the rest of the family. We cried together and mourned. At eighteen and twenty-two, we were still just kids, trying to figure out an outlet for that pain.

Just a few weeks later, I found out Joe was shooting up heroin. I had no idea what to do. How do you handle that, especially when you're barely an adult yourself? I took him shopping to confront him about it, because I knew he wouldn't react badly if we were in public. Standing there in the middle of the mall, I asked him, "You shootin' up, man?" He immediately went into lies, denial, and shame. But I knew. "Let me see your arms, then," I said, and he refused.

That was all the answer I needed. I took him home, and he spent the next few days withdrawing on my couch. I can still picture that couch clearly in my mind—pale pink-orange with a pattern of tiny white flowers, my brother's body laid out on it. If you're lucky, you've never seen somebody withdraw. It's intense and painful. For three or four solid days, he writhed in pain, sweating through his clothes, and had microseizures. His body shook and itched unbearably, but he endured.

After, I sat him down for some tough love. "I still love you," I told him. "I'm never going to stop loving you. Shit happens. Come on, let's pick up the pieces." That's what we did, and for a few years, he did so well. He stayed with me for a few more months, then moved to North Carolina to live with our uncle, who taught him to do AV work for live events. He loved his job and even got to meet Bill Clinton and Steven Tyler from Aerosmith because of it. He went back to school and was halfway to earning his bachelor's degree.

Eventually, though, opioids came back into his life. I don't know for certain how it happened, but I know he broke his hand and foot, and I have a feeling he was prescribed opioids for pain management. Once again, I can't help but think, *What if he had been offered cannabis instead?* He tried—he tried *so hard*—to stay clean, so many times, but he was stuck in the cycle of addiction, a cycle that had started at just fourteen years old. Before he had a chance to grow up, his future and what should have been some of the best years of his life were stolen from him.

This is the consequence of the stigma of cannabis, and my brother's story isn't unique. In 2017, an estimated 1.7 million people in the United States suffered from substance use disorders related to prescription opioid pain relievers.[2]

BREAKING *ALL* THE STIGMAS

This is a book about cannabis, yet in writing it, I quickly discovered that I could not write about the stigma of cannabis without also writing about other stigmas that intersect and connect with cannabis—specifically, the stigmas around addiction and race.

There's a stigma that addicts are bad people who have made decisions that destroyed their life. As a family member of an addict, I can understand the inclination to think that, even as I know it's not true. Loving an addict is an

---

[2] Center for Behavioral Health Statistics and Quality (CBHSQ), *2017 National Survey on Drug Use and Health: Detailed Tables* (Rockville, MD: Substance Abuse and Mental Health Services Administration, 2018), https://www.drugabuse.gov/drug-topics/opioids/opioid-overdose-crisis.

emotional roller coaster. You don't know what's wrong. Then you find out it's drugs. So, you try to get them help. Sometimes they resist. Sometimes they try. They pick up the pieces, only to fall off the wagon again. It feels like a never-ending cycle, with no clear path out. You have to straddle the line of wanting to help, while still holding the addict accountable. You have to endure the hurt of seeing your loved one act like someone else—someone mean and selfish, who says and does hurtful things. They may steal from you and burn all their bridges.

As difficult as it can be as a family member to love an addict and see past their addiction, I think it's even more difficult for the addict. For twenty years, my brother struggled with feelings of shame and worthlessness. He believed the stigma. He believed that he was a bad person, that his addiction was his fault, and that he didn't deserve love. That broke my heart more than anything else. When I told him I was writing this book and explained the societal circumstances that had contributed to his addiction—the stigma against cannabis and how that led to opioids being the only option presented for pain management—he was able to shed some of that shame. He still had to be accountable for his actions in the present, but he was able to stop blaming himself for his addiction, for taking half of a pill at just fourteen years old.

A lot of people are in the cannabis industry for financial reasons. I don't think there's anything wrong with that. One of my big goals with this book is to help you make more money. But I also think that we are more fulfilled and successful in business when we have a purpose deeper than money alone. In breaking the stigma against cannabis, we can also break the stigma against addiction. We can stop perpetuating a system that creates addicts and then blames them for their addiction. We can try to save lives, in the most literal sense.

As cannabis retailers, we also have the opportunity—and responsibility—to break stigmas around race. The stigma against cannabis has racist roots, and for nearly one hundred years, cannabis has been used against people of color as a method to criminalize and incarcerate them. Breaking the stigma against cannabis means educating people that cannabis is not dangerous or bad in most circumstances. We cannot do that without acknowledging that people of color have been wrongly labeled as criminals and disproportionately harmed for selling or simply using cannabis. Now, as more states legalize cannabis, people (who are almost always white) are making millions doing something that got people of color thrown in jail. It's not fair, it's not just, and it's our duty to elevate people of color in the industry. Beyond simply acknowledging these truths, we need to take *action* to right these wrongs.

It's all connected for me: cannabis, addiction, racism. I went to a high school where there was a desegregation policy still in place where a large percentage of my class were people of color, and many of my friends were Black. My white friends and I were called "wiggers," the derogatory term for white people who crossed racial friendship lines and embraced Black culture. As a poor kid, growing up in a bad neighborhood, it was far easier to relate to Black people than many of my white peers. I feel a little uncomfortable writing this, because if you look at me today, you would see a privileged white woman, and I don't want to equate my struggles with those of people of color. At the same time, I want to acknowledge how important and impactful Black culture, particularly Black music, was on me as a child whose family life was shaped by addiction. When hip-hop artists like Tupac and Bone Thugs-N-Harmony sang of their struggles—of being poor, of living surrounded by violence, of loved ones dying too soon—I was able to hear my own pain. Then, when Eminem came on the scene, I felt seen in a way I never had before. Here was a man who had seen the pain of addiction in his family, just like me. We were just poor white trailer trash trying to find a way out.

Talking about these things matters. It helps us to feel less alone, and with an open conversation and proper education, we can begin breaking all the stigmas—the stigma against cannabis, the stigma against addiction, and the racist stigma against people of color, particularly Black people. These are lofty goals, but we can do it, all while simultaneously building profitable, competitive businesses. The truth is, in securing a cannabis license, you haven't won the lottery. You've won an opportunity. It's the opportunity of a lifetime, but it also comes with responsibilities. So let's become better retailers and break the stigmas.

Chapter 1

THE STIGMA AGAINST CANNABIS: WHERE IT CAME FROM AND WHAT IT'S COST US

The vast majority of US adults support the legalization of cannabis, with 60 percent supporting legalization for medical and recreational use, and 31 percent supporting medical use only. Only *8 percent* say it should not be legal for use by adults in any scenario.[3] These numbers are promising for those of us in the industry, but behind the numbers, many stigmas still exist.

---

[3] Ted Van Green, "Americans Overwhelmingly Say Marijuana Should Be Legal for Recreational or Medical Use," Pew Research Center, April 16, 2021, https://www.pewresearch.org/fact-tank/2021/04/16/americans-overwhelmingly-say-marijuana-should-be-legal-for-recreational-or-medical-use/.

For nearly one hundred years, a PR campaign has been waged against cannabis. Though public opinion is now shifting, it will take time to undo the decades of lies and misinformation. To help you understand what we are up against, I want to take you back to 2008. Barack Obama had just won the presidential election, and an initiative for medical marijuana passed in Michigan, with 63 percent in favor. Individuals were now allowed to grow their own cannabis for medical use, and caregivers were allowed to grow cannabis for up to five patients, with a maximum of seventy-two plants.

Now meet Mike. Mike worked as a general contractor in Michigan and was a long-term cannabis user. In many instances, blue-collar laborers do not have access to traditional healthcare. Given the physical toll of their jobs, many, like Mike, self-medicate with cannabis to ease their aches and pains. With medical marijuana legalized and a recent leg injury that had confined him to his home, Mike began cultivating cannabis. Then, in 2010, he started a clinic where people could come and get the certification that allowed them to possess cannabis.

Mike saw the occasional twenty-something who wanted an MMJ (medical marijuana) card as a path to recreational use but, mostly, he saw people desperate for pain management and treatment for other qualifying conditions under Michigan state law. He saw cancer patients who wanted cannabis to manage their symptoms. He saw individuals in such debilitating pain that they needed wheelchairs to maneuver through the world. He saw uninsured individuals who couldn't afford traditional healthcare procedures or prescription medication and just wanted *something* to manage their pain.

Unfortunately, the laws in Michigan were gray. While medical use had been legalized, there was not a clear path to *selling* cannabis. The law did not explicitly ban dispensaries, but neither did it create a path to opening one. So even after getting an MMJ card, many patients could not actually get cannabis, unless they grew the plants themselves (which was not feasible for everyone) or happened to know a caregiver. Seeing this need for product and accessibility—and unaware of the legal issues—Mike decided to open a dispensary in 2013.

Six months later, in 2014, Michigan State Police officers, decked out in SWAT-like gear, stormed both Mike's house and the dispensary. Mike's staff were handcuffed and forced to sit on the ground for hours as officers searched the property. The police ultimately seized Mike's car as well as everything in his bank account.

Everyone was hit with felony charges. After fighting the charges and taking a plea deal, Mike's final conviction was possession of two grams, or approximately three walnut-sized buds. Fortunately, he didn't go to prison—although if his skin color were different, this would likely be a different story. Still, it was a felony, which makes gaining meaningful employment exponentially more difficult.

Though cannabis is now legal both medically and recreationally in Michigan, Mike still has a felony on his record. For two grams of cannabis. Some states are looking at automatic expungement for cannabis offenses, but under the current laws in Michigan, as of 2020, you have to hire a lawyer to get your record expunged, which can cost thousands of dollars. Mike is in the privileged position where he could afford to do that if needed, but many others are not. If you require people to hire a lawyer (or the process is so complicated that it's incredibly difficult without a lawyer), you've created a pay-to-play system that will disproportionately impact people of color, who are more likely to not be able to afford a lawyer due to systemic wealth and income inequalities.

Mike's entire life was upended following the raids, and it took him years to pick the pieces back up again. Everything in his head said he was doing the right thing by cultivating and selling cannabis for pain-management purposes. After all, medical use was legalized, and he was helping people. From the Michigan State Police's perspective, due to the legal gray area, he was doing wrong, and they were doing their jobs. However, I have to believe there were more heinous crimes to pursue.

The point I'm trying to make here is that despite legalization and majority support of medical cannabis, a huge stigma remained. These raids occurred less than seven years ago, and six years after medical marijuana was passed in Michigan. The percentage of the Michigan population that supported medical marijuana in 2008 is approximately the same as the percentage of the US population that supports medical and recreational use today: 60 percent. There are thousands of individuals with a similar story to Mike's. As such stories show, as great as those numbers seem, they don't mean that we're not still up against challenges as an industry. We are. Despite widespread public acceptance, rules and regulations significantly lag behind, ultimately delaying consumer accessibility. There remain large pockets of this country continuing to use cannabis as a tool to create new criminals.

Breaking the stigma against cannabis is the responsibility of each and every individual currently working in the cannabis industry. In particular for those of us working in retail, we are on the front lines of changing the criminal and negative perceptions associated with cannabis. As front-line workers, it is important to understand how the stigma against cannabis came about and how it has harmed not just the cannabis industry and cannabis users, but our entire country. We've all been lied to. These *Big Lies* have shaped our beliefs about race, cannabis, and addiction, and it's time to unmask these Big Lies for what they are: *lies*.

BIG LIE #1:
BLACK MEN ARE DANGEROUS

The lie that Black men are inherently dangerous extends far, far back into our country's history, but we're going to start in the 1930s, with a man named Harry J. Anslinger. Anslinger became the commissioner of the Federal Bureau of Narcotics in 1930. He was "so racist that he was regarded as a crazy racist in the 1920s."[4] He frequently used the N-word in official police memos, and he's responsible for targeting and harassing Billie Holiday for singing the song "Strange Fruit," about lynchings.

Anslinger initially spent most of his time chasing down bootleggers. When Prohibition ended in 1933, he suddenly found himself out of a job. For the Federal Bureau of Narcotics to continue to have purpose—and receive the funding that paid his salary—Anslinger had to find a new bogeyman to prosecute. He chose marijuana, a term which itself has racist roots and was a way to otherize cannabis as a "Mexican drug." At this time, cannabis was not regulated in any way in the United States, so he first had to make it illegal. In order to do that, he needed people to fear it. He figured, why not link it to something people already fear? Black people, particularly Black men.

And so, the propaganda began. Anslinger sparked a national anti-cannabis movement by tying cannabis usage to the Black community and other marginalized groups. "Reefer makes darkies think they're as good as white men," Anslinger was quoted as saying. "There are one hundred thousand total marijuana smokers in the US, and most are Negroes, Hispanics,

---

4 Ramtin Arablouei and Rund Abdelfatah, "Looking Back at Jazz Singer Billie Holiday's Influence on American Music," *All Things Considered*, NPR, August 22, 2019, https://www.npr.org/2019/08/22/7534 93982/looking-back-at-jazz-singer-billie-holidays-influence-on-american-music.

Filipinos, and entertainers. Their Satanic music, jazz and swing, result from marijuana use. This marijuana causes white women to seek sexual relations with Negroes, entertainers, and any others."[5] Considering that fourteen-year-old Emmett Till was brutally killed for allegedly flirting with or whistling at a white woman in 1955, you can imagine how effective this messaging was. Few things scared American people as much as the idea of Black men sleeping with white women.

Obviously, Anslinger didn't invent racism, but his propaganda propagated and amplified it. He also institutionalized a method to criminalize and persecute Black people and other minorities through the War on Drugs. He led the Federal Bureau of Narcotics until 1962, and there is no doubt in my mind that during his more than thirty-year tenure, his racism cascaded down through the bureau. He directly and indirectly created much of the institutionalized racism that exists today, manifesting itself in the form of mass incarceration and police brutality. I actually own a small relic of his racist campaign—a Reefer Madness magnet I picked up many years ago while traveling—that depicts a devil that not so coincidentally looks like a Black man.

In short, Anslinger used the lie that Black men are dangerous to help make cannabis illegal, and then he weaponized cannabis against minority communities. It's a strategy many politicians, including Richard Nixon, have since used. John Ehrlichman, counsel to Nixon and assistant to the president for domestic affairs, once said:

---

[5] Laura Smith, "How a Racist Hate-Monger Masterminded America's War on Drugs," Timeline, February 27, 2018, https://timeline.com/harry-anslinger-racist-war-on-drugs-prison-industrial-complex-fb5cbc28 1189.

The Nixon campaign in 1968, and the Nixon White House after that, had two enemies: the antiwar left and Black people. You understand what I'm saying? We knew we couldn't make it illegal to be either against the [Vietnam] war or Black, but by getting the public to associate the hippies with marijuana and Blacks with heroin, and then criminalizing both heavily, we could disrupt those communities. We could arrest their leaders, raid their homes, break up their meetings, and vilify them night after night on the evening news. Did we know we were lying about the drugs? Of course we did.[6]

People of color are disproportionately impacted by the War on Drugs to this day. According to an ACLU report, there were more than 6.1 million cannabis arrests between 2010 to 2018. The vast majority of these arrests—nine out of every ten, to be specific—were for possession, and though Black and white people use cannabis at similar rates, a Black person is 3.64 times more likely to be arrested for possession.[7] Hispanic and other racial minorities almost certainly face disparities in arrest rates as well, but due to the way certain data is collected and reported, it is more difficult to determine specific statistics for these groups.

Black men—and racial minorities as a whole—are not dangerous. As industry professionals, we need to understand the racist roots behind the stigma of cannabis and do our part to elevate those groups disproportionately and unfairly impacted by the War on Drugs.

---

[6] Dan Baum, "Legalize It All," *Harper's Magazine*, April 2016, https://harpers.org/archive/2016/04 /legalize-it-all.

[7] ACLU, *A Tale of Two Countries: Racially Targeted Arrests in the Era of Marijuana Reform*, ACLU Research Report, 2020, https://www.aclu.org/report/tale-two-countries-racially-targeted-arrests-era -marijuana-reform.

Q&A with Betty Mitchell, CEO of Tively

Betty Mitchell is a cannabis entrepreneur from California who owns Liveade Wellness and Tively, and she was the first graduate of the Sacramento CORE (Cannabis Opportunity Reinvestment and Equity) program. She graciously agreed to share her thoughts about cannabis for this book—from the stigma of cannabis, to her experience as a Black woman in the industry, to advice for minority owners and cannabis retailers in general. You will find several sidebars featuring her wisdom.

Q:

What has been your experience with the stigma of cannabis?

A:

Growing up in Arkansas, if you talked about cannabis, you might as well have been talking about heroin. At that time, a lot of Vietnam vets were coming home and getting addicted to heroin, which was horrible, and cannabis was put on that same level. Still today, people put cannabis in the same category as meth or heroin, when it isn't even in the same ballpark.

I think some of it is connected to the religious front, as the stigma seems the worst to me in the southern Bible Belt states. But it's all smoke and mirrors. These are the states where people preach against sex but then they're the number one online porn consumers in the United States. If God comes back, they think she'll take out San Francisco or New York first, but I think she's going to take the southern Bible Belt states.

People will slowly come around, though, once they need it themselves. When you're in pain, it's amazing how the mind will shift and reposition cannabis.

Q: How did the war on drugs impact your community?

I can remember people getting stopped for whatever reason, and then the cops would find a little joint on them. Just a joint was enough to send you to jail for three or four weeks at a time. That might not seem long, but it was long enough to lose your job, and once you lost your job, it took you down quicker than anything. If you were married and had two kids, it would take the whole family down. And God help you if you had an eighth bag, because that could get you serious jail time—two or three years. That kind of thing followed you, not only affecting your ability to get a job, but also giving you a stigma in the community. Jail and prison are two very different things, but if you went to jail, people treated it just like you'd gone to prison. It was a double dip—you had the cops and the entire system working against you, and then your own community could be pretty unforgiving, labeling you a drug addict.

BIG LIE #2:
CANNABIS IS DANGEROUS

Using fear of Black men, Anslinger convinced people that cannabis was dangerous. He reinforced and disseminated this lie with the Gore Files, a collection of two hundred violent crimes, including armed robbery, assault, and murder, that Anslinger claimed were due to cannabis usage. One of the most famous was the Licata killings in 1933, in which Victor Licata murdered his parents and three siblings with an ax. According to Anslinger, he did so under the influence of cannabis. A year prior to the killings, though, police had tried to commit Licata due to mental illness. The Licata murders were undoubtedly tragic, but all facts point to mental illness as the cause, not cannabis.[8]

Despite this, Anslinger spun these and other such stories to fit his purpose. The criminals highlighted in these stories were designed to prey on people's fears, with perpetrators including child rapists as well as Black, Hispanic, lesbian, and other minority groups that were wrongly discriminated against. Anslinger catapulted these stories to a national level with the help of William Randolph Hearst, who owned several "yellow journalism" (aka fake news) newspapers across the country that focused on sensationalization as opposed to factual reporting.

In a hearing that led to the Marihuana Tax Act of 1937—the first regulation of cannabis in the country—Anslinger stood in front of Congress and listed case after case of violent crimes, attributing them to cannabis usage. He even went so far as to say that "one [cannabis] cigarette might develop a homicidal mania," and he claimed that "all the experts agree that the continued use leads to insanity."[9] These were blatant lies. In fact, twenty-nine of thirty representatives from the American Medical Association objected to his proposed ban of cannabis.[10] Anslinger, however, routinely rejected any evidence that contradicted his claims, calling it "unscientific."

---

[8] Paul Guzzo, "An Ybor City Ax Murderer Led to Marijuana Regulation. Now There's a Movie in the Works," *Tampa Bay Times*, May 14, 2020, https://www.tampabay.com/arts-entertainment/arts /movies/2020/05/14/an-ybor-city-ax-murderer-led-to-marijuana-regulation-now-theres-a-movie -in-the-works/.

[9] *Taxation of Marihuana: Hearing on H.R. 6906, Before a Subcommittee of the Committee on Finance*, 75th Cong. 14 (1937) (statement of H. J. Anslinger, Commissioner of Narcotics), https://www.finance.senate. gov/download/taxation-of-marihuana-subcommittee-on-hr-6906.

[10] Natalie Papillion, "Reefer Madness: The Brief and Wondrous Life of Pot Prohibition, Pt. I," Medium, January 31, 2020, https://medium.com/equityorg/reefer-madness-the-brief-and-wondrous-life-of-pot -prohibition-pt-1-2872ffb17bc4.

Of those two hundred cases listed in the Gore Files, guess how many were properly attributed to cannabis usage? *Zero.* That's right. Researchers later found that 198 of the 200 crimes were wrongly attributed to cannabis usage, and the remaining two cases were entirely fictional.[11] At the time, though, with no internet or mass communication, it was all too easy for Anslinger to propagate these lies as truth.

The idea that cannabis makes people dangerous is ludicrous to me. I grew up during the War on Drugs, and I bought into many of the lies. I truly believed cannabis was bad, but never once did I think of cannabis users as dangerous. As a child, I spent time around both alcoholics and cannabis users, and the difference was clear to me. Drunk people were violent, abusive, and dangerous. High people were safe, normal, and most importantly not violent.

Over the years, as it became blatantly clear that cannabis does not turn people into violent criminals, the stigma shifted. Cannabis was attached to the hippie movement and linked to "subversive" behavior, like not supporting the Vietnam War or rejecting puritanical views of sex. Anything that went against social norms was considered dangerous, and so cannabis was still branded evil, with cannabis users being labeled as stinky, dirty, lazy stoners—a stigma that, in many ways, continues to this day.

In the drug education I received, I learned that all drugs are fundamentally bad, with no differentiation. Cannabis, meth, heroin, LSD, cocaine—they were all grouped together. Maybe you remember the 1980s commercial of a frying egg, with the tagline "This is your brain on drugs." Not "This is your brain on crack" or "This is your brain on heroin." These ads were well-intentioned, but when a bunch of different substances are grouped together under one blanket term, a true education is not provided.

---

[11] Ibid.

Even when people acknowledged that cannabis was less harmful and addictive than harder drugs, they emphasized that it was still incredibly dangerous because it was a "gateway drug." As a child, I honestly believed that if I smoked cannabis, it would only be a matter of time until I was shooting up heroin in an alley. According to the National Institute on Drug Abuse, though, "The majority of people who use marijuana do not go on to use other, 'harder' substances."[12]

Today, despite all the evidence that cannabis is safe for most people, the lie persists. Cannabis is classified as a Schedule I drug, meaning it has "no currently accepted medical use and a high potential for abuse."[13] Other Schedule I drugs include heroin and meth. In 2018 alone, there were almost seven hundred thousand cannabis arrests, accounting for more than 43 percent of all drug arrests, and according to the FBI, police made more cannabis arrests than for all violent crimes combined that year.[14] As a country, it's long past time that we focused our attention on true dangers. As a cannabis retailer, it's important to recognize that even though *you* know cannabis is not dangerous, your customers might not.

BIG LIE #3:
OPIOIDS ARE SAFE

Because of the lie that cannabis is dangerous, it was not normalized (or legal) as a method of pain management. There was a need for pain management,

---

[12] National Institute on Drug Abuse, "Is Marijuana a Gateway Drug?" July 2020, https://www.drugabuse.gov/publications/research-reports/marijuana/marijuana-gateway-drug.

[13] DEA, "Drug Scheduling," accessed May 6, 2021, https://www.dea.gov/drug-information/drug-scheduling.

[14] ACLU, *A Tale of Two Countries.*

though, and so in 1996, Purdue Pharma, under the direction of the Sackler family, developed and patented OxyContin. It was hailed as a miracle drug that took all the pain away, as if by magic. Magic often comes at a cost, though, and in this case, the cost was hundreds of thousands of American lives—more than five hundred thousand to be specific.[15] In my opinion, Purdue Pharma essentially took a cousin of heroin, put it in a pill, and spent enough money to make the whole world think it was safe. Nothing could be further from the truth.

The Sacklers' motive in creating OxyContin had seemingly little, if anything, to do with altruism and everything to do with greed. When OxyContin made its debut, Richard Sackler, then a company executive, said the drug would bring "a blizzard of prescriptions that will bury the competition."[16] That's exactly what happened, due to an aggressive marketing campaign driven by the Sackler family, particularly Richard Sackler. The drug went on to generate $35 billion in revenue.[17]

Within a few years, evidence emerged that the drug was addictive and led to overdose deaths. While we were all being told that cannabis was the gateway drug, Purdue Pharma was flooding our country with the real gateway drug—opioids. They funded research studies that supported the use of OxyContin, and Richard Sackler put intense pressure on sales managers to sell more.[18] To meet Sackler's demands, sales representatives focused

---

[15] Harriet Ryan, "Review: A New Exposé Is an Air-Tight Indictment of the Family behind the Opioid Crisis," *Los Angeles Times*, April 13, 2021, https://www.latimes.com/entertainment-arts/books /story/2021-04-13/review-the-family-that-crippled-america-the-sacklers-get-a-full-biography.

[16] Andrew Joseph, "'A Blizzard of Prescriptions': Documents Reveal New Details about Purdue's Marketing of OxyContin, STAT, January 15, 2019, https://www.statnews.com/2019/01/15/massachusetts -purdue-lawsuit-new-details/.

[17] Patrick Radden Keefe, *Empire of Pain* (New York: Doubleday, 2021), 4.

[18] *The Crime of the Century*, part 1, directed, produced, and written by Alex Gibney, released May 10, 2021, on HBO, https://www.hbo.com/documentaries/the-crime-of-the-century.

their efforts on high-volume doctors and pushed doctors to prescribe high doses—both of which increased addiction rates.[19] The company even created a rap video to push their sales reps into selling their newest opioid.[20] While Black people were being thrown in prison simply for possession of cannabis, Purdue Pharma was appropriating Black culture and music to legally push a more addictive drug. A Black man never would have gotten away with what the Sacklers did. Only a white family with generational wealth could have pulled this Big Lie off.

This Big Lie has harmed hundreds of thousands of Americans. As just one example of many, my friend Jeanne's boyfriend, Tommy, was hit by a car, and his doctor prescribed him opioids to manage the pain. Medical cannabis had not yet been legalized in Florida at the time, so cannabis wasn't even presented to him as an option. It was only a matter of time before he became addicted. As we'll discuss further in the next section, this didn't make him less of a person, like many often think of an addict.

As overdose deaths increased and the dangers of opioids came to light, doctors began cutting off patients like Tommy. I don't disagree with the decision to rein in the distribution of opioids, but in Tommy's case and many others, because he still had pain and no alternatives, he took to the streets to manage his pain and addiction. The drugs on the street are not lab tested, nor do they go through the rigorous manufacturing process of pharmaceutical-grade medications. Many street drugs are mixed with dangerous fentanyl and even carfentanil, which is an elephant tranquilizer. One day Tommy was given a bad batch, and he overdosed and transitioned from this world.

---

[19] *The Crime of the Century.*

[20] Jessica Glenza, "Opioid Manufacturers Made Parody Rap Videos to Help Push Products," *Guardian*, December 7, 2019, https://www.theguardian.com/us-news/2019/dec/07/opiod-makers-music-videos-sales.

When a loved one dies, all you want to do is grieve, but there are so many things to do. You have to tell family and friends what happened, reliving the event over and over again. You spend every moment analyzing what brought you to that moment. In the case of an overdose victim, you analyze what you didn't do to save them. Then you have to make phone calls and funeral arrangements. You have to close cell phone accounts and put clothes away. All of this is extremely overwhelming, not to mention dealing with the pure shock of death itself.

Looking at Jeanne and Tommy, the hardest factor of it all was that they had a beautiful three-year-old daughter, Nikki. We all called her Spicy due to her precocious attitude. Understanding the overwhelming burden Jeanne was facing, I offered to take Nikki for a week when Tommy died. "Spicy and I will be fine," I told her. During that time, I pretended like nothing had happened, and we spent the week having fun. The night before Nikki went home, we watched *Frozen*. She was so happy. As I held her in my arms, I couldn't help tearing up knowing that the next day she was going to find out her daddy was gone, and her little life was going to change forever. All I could do was hold her tighter, wishing things were different than they were.

Nikki is six now, and she's not as spicy as she was. A couple of weeks ago, she was holding my hand and said to me, "Aunt Char, did you know that my dad's dead?" I squeezed her hand and said, "Yeah, honey, I know." Someday, Jeanne will have to explain to Nikki what happened, and Nikki will have to face and come to terms with Tommy's story.

Opioids destroy lives, and the ripples extend beyond the addict alone. Nikki is one of hundreds of thousands of children who are going to have to develop an image of their parent who was erased from their life because of opioids. An entire generation of children will be shaped by addiction and the absence of their parents. What do we tell these children? Should we let them believe their mom or dad was bad because they were a drug addict? It is a fundamental disservice to the deceased to not speak the truth to how and why these deaths occur. These deaths are caused by misinformation fed to our public health servants.

Today, we have more knowledge about opioids and the potential for addiction, and we have terms like the "Opioid Crisis" and the "Opioid Epidemic" to describe the wide-ranging impact of this Big Lie. "Crisis" fails to do the situation justice, though. The scale is magnitudes greater than a crisis. I don't know one, two, or three people who died from this. I genuinely can't count on two hands how many people I know who were lost to opioids. Opioids roared through my rural southwestern Michigan community like a freight train. No one saw it coming. Looking back, we didn't understand at the time why these deaths suddenly started happening. Oxys were every-where. Then people started getting addicted, then dying.

These people have names. Many of them were my peers from high school. I went to their funerals. I hugged their moms, dads, sisters, brothers, chil-dren, and friends. I have watched some of their children grow into adults without their mother or father. An entire generation is being robbed of their parents. I have looked into the eyes of survivors and seen the pain. I feel it.

Derrick Thompson died in the bathroom of an airport on his way to a clean house out of state. Emily Johnson died in her bed after a small moment of weakness after being clean for five months. Aunt Sheila lost her boys Joey and Chucky Stevens. The day before Joey died, she begged the doctor to not prescribe him additional pills. Brad woke up next to his girlfriend who had died in her sleep. Bobby was riding his bike, then sat down and just went to sleep. A single mishap or series of mishaps should not equate to a death sentence, especially when the problem was created by the lie that this medication was safe. Our pharmaceutical model created this illness and has continued to perpetuate the *systemic creation of new addicts*, resulting in the subsequent increase in deaths related to overdoses.

I started seeing these deaths in 2001, when I was nineteen. Twenty years later, the list grows each and every single year. So no, "crisis" doesn't adequately describe it for me. "Epidemic" isn't quite right either, as an epidemic implies a disease that is infectious. I think it's best called the "Opioid Endemic." Per the CDC, "endemic" refers to "the constant presence and/or usual prevalence of a disease or infectious agent in a population within a geographic area."[21] That's what we're dealing with: a disease that is not going away and that has very clear borders. Other countries do not suffer from the propensity of opioid-related deaths the way the United States does. In 2018, the European Union estimated 8,317 overdose deaths, or 22.3 deaths per million of the population aged 15–64, while the United States had 67,367, or 207 deaths per million (these numbers are total overdose deaths, but the overwhelming percentage are due to opioids).[22] Even taking into account the fact that some EU countries likely underreport, that is a huge discrepancy. If you are reading this, you very likely live here in the United States. This is our problem, and it is our job to solve it.

There is no clear end in sight for the Opioid Endemic. It was big news for a while, but then it faded into the background. You can only watch so many mothers cry over their children before you become numb, and if you believe the next Big Lie, you think their son or daughter was fundamentally flawed for being an addict anyway. I know it's difficult to keep caring about

---

[21] CDC, "Lesson 1: Introduction to Epidemiology," last reviewed May 18, 2012, https://www.cdc.gov/csels/dsepd/ss1978/lesson1/section11.html.

[22] Thomas Seyler, Isabelle Giraudon, André Noor, Jane Mounteney, and Paul Griffiths, "Is Europe Facing an Opioid Epidemic: What Does European Monitoring Data Tell Us?," *European Journal of Pain* 25, no. 5 (2021): 1072–80, https://doi.org/10.1002/ejp.1728.

a problem when we're constantly bombarded by new issues that need attention too, but as long as people are dying, we have to keep talking about the Opioid Endemic. I can turn on my radio and hear a PSA about how smoking cigarettes or vaping is going to make my legs fall off, but I've never heard a PSA about opioids triggering a disease called addiction or about carfentanil hitting the streets and wiping out young people. Can we please change this narrative?

You may not be personally connected to the Opioid Endemic in the way I am, but as a cannabis retailer, you are in the business of pain management. By understanding this Big Lie and providing people with an alternative to addictive opioids, you could literally save lives.

BIG LIE #4:
ADDICTION IS THE ADDICT'S FAULT

I understand the impulse to blame addiction on the addict. An addict's struggles with addiction can be enough to tear their loved ones apart inside. You want to scream, "Why can't you just quit?" But blaming addiction on the addict makes as much sense as blaming someone for having cancer, asthma, or migraines.

Here's the thing: no one wants to be an addict. *No one.* As the US Department of Health and Human Services has declared, addiction is *not* a moral failing or the result of a character flaw.[23] Addiction is a disease of the brain, and per the US National Library of Medicine, "Opioids have a high potential

---

[23] US Department of Health and Human Services (HHS), *Facing Addiction in America: The Surgeon General's Spotlight on Opioids* (Washington, DC: HHS, 2018).

for causing addiction in some people, even when the medications are prescribed appropriately and taken as directed."[24]

Opioids affect people differently. Some people can take opioids and get off of them easily. Others cannot. We don't know exactly why, but some people cannot control their bodies' attachment to the drug, not because they are bad people, but because of the composition of their bodies and brains. It's no different from how some people have type 1 diabetes, and others don't. For some people, taking an opioid flips a switch in their brain. Continuing to use is not a choice; it's a compulsion that feels as strong as the drive to breathe or eat.

Addiction has to start *somewhere*, though, right? Maybe we can't blame addicts for *being* addicted, but we can blame them for *getting* addicted in the first place. It's not that simple. Is it fair to blame my brother, Joe, for getting addicted when he was only fourteen years old, taking a pill his stepdad had given him? Absolutely not. He never had a chance to not get addicted.

Many of us were taught "Just say no." The idea was that some drug dealer was going to find us in the parking lot and offer us drugs, and all we had to do was say no. I don't know about you, but no stranger (or even acquaintance) has ever come up and offered me drugs. That's not how it works, especially with opioids. It comes from a trusted source. It comes from your parent, your doctor, your friend. Joe went through the D.A.R.E. program. If someone had offered him cannabis, he would have said no because he'd been taught that cannabis was "bad." But no one prepared him to deal with a trusted adult offering him something dangerous.

Every single person I know who got addicted received their first pill or hit from a trusted source. My stepdad and Tommy both got it from their

---

[24] "Opioid Addiction," MedlinePlus, last updated August 18, 2020, https://medlineplus.gov/genetics/condition/opioid-addiction/.

doctors. My brother Joe got it from our stepdad. My hilarious friend Brandi, who has been clean and sober since July 19, 2015, was given heroin, on Christmas, by her mom, who first got addicted to opioids prescribed by her doctor before moving on to heroin. This is how the Opioid Endemic started. It didn't start with irresponsible drug dealers on the street. It started between patients and doctors. Opioids moved through our world via trusted sources.

Why do I mention the date of Brandi's sobriety? Brandi was my best friend Jenna's sister and my idol. I knew her before addiction. Cried about losing her to it. Then celebrated getting her back. I congratulate her for this milestone in her recovery. If someone in recovery tells you how long they have been clean and sober, take the time to congratulate them, because it is a powerful and noteworthy achievement.

Addicts are put into the category of scum. They are seen as lowlifes, junkies, criminals, less than human, and unworthy of love. That's how the Sacklers apparently saw them. "We have to hammer on the abusers in every way possible," Richard Sackler wrote in an email in February 2001. "They are the culprits and the problem. They are reckless criminals."[25] He also said, "Why should they be entitled to our sympathies?"[26] The Sacklers crafted a narrative that fit their self-serving motives in the same way Anslinger did. That they could be so callous and blame the addicts—the victims of their profit-hungry practices—is astounding to me.

---

[25] Joseph, "A Blizzard of Prescriptions."

[26] Ryan, "Review: A New Exposé."

It's easy to blame the addict, but it's not right. Don't get me wrong, the behavior of an active addict is so difficult to deal with. I have blamed them for their disease. I've been angry. They are very hard to love with all the lies, deceptions, and letdowns. It has taken me my entire life, but after watching, reading, listening, and searching for answers, I finally understand. *At the onset of addiction, addicts cannot control their disease.* If they could, they would not be addicts. No one chooses that path. Addicts are still accountable for their actions. As I would tell my brother, "You're accountable for yourself today. *Live one day at a time.*" Accountability is achieved when they find recovery. It's an addict's job to stay clean, which is a daily fight and struggle, but their *addiction* is not their fault.

Who is responsible for addiction, then? The people who caused the Opioid Endemic, people like the Sackler family. As Patrick Radden Keefe puts it in *Empire of Pain*, "Prior to the introduction of OxyContin, America did not have an opioid crisis. After the introduction of OxyContin, it did."[27] While heroin had been around for years, impacting low-income communities, the introduction of OxyContin significantly exacerbated America's dependence on opioids for pain management.

There's no question in my mind that the Sacklers and Purdue Pharma created the Opioid Endemic. There is even empirical evidence. In 2019, a team of economists released a study looking at the connection between Purdue Pharma's marketing of OxyContin and overdose deaths. When OxyContin was first released, five states (California, Idaho, Illinois, New York, and Texas) had "triplicate" programs, which meant every time doctors wanted to prescribe Schedule II narcotics, they had to fill out special triplicate prescription forms and file one copy with the state (the idea being

---

[27] Keefe, *Empire of Pain*, 5.

that state agencies could then maintain a prescription database to monitor for irregularities). As indicated in internal documents (available as a result of litigation), Purdue Pharma chose not to market heavily in these states during the initial launch of OxyContin because they believed these state's doctors were less likely to prescribe the drug, due to the extra paperwork and not wanting to be monitored by the state.

By comparing these five states to the rest of the country, we can better understand the impact of OxyContin and, specifically, Purdue's heavy marketing tactics. According to the study, OxyContin distribution was about 50 percent lower in triplicate states. Prior to 1996, these states actually had higher overdose death rates compared to nontriplicate states, but following the introduction of OxyContin in 1996, the relationship flipped. Nontriplicate states saw substantially slower growth in overdose deaths, and overall, the study's authors estimate that "nontriplicate states would have had an average of 36 percent fewer drug overdose deaths and 44 percent fewer opioid overdose deaths in 1996–2017 if they had been triplicate states."[28]

Over the years, Purdue Pharma has come under intense scrutiny for their role in the Opioid Endemic, and in 2019, facing thousands of lawsuits, the company filed for bankruptcy. In 2021, they agreed to a bankruptcy settlement in which the Sacklers will pay approximately $4.5 billion.[29] While $4.5 billion sounds like a lot of money, it's a drop in the bucket compared to the cost of the Opioid Endemic, estimated at more than $2 trillion by

[28] Abby E. Alpert, William N. Evans, Ethan M.J. Lieber, and David Powell, "Origins of the Opioid Crisis and Its Enduring Impacts" (National Bureau of Economic Research Working Paper Series, no. 26500, November 2019), https://www.nber.org/papers/w26500.

[29] Jan Hoffman, "Purdue Pharma Is Dissolved and Sacklers Pay $4.5 Billion to Settle Opioid Claims," *New York Times*, September 1, 2021, updated September 17, 2021, https://www.nytimes.com/2021/09/01/health/purdue-sacklers-opioids-settlement.html.

the states involved in the lawsuit.[30] What's more, from 2008 to 2017, the Sackler family withdrew more than $10 billion from Purdue Pharma, and with an agreement to pay the $4.5 billion over nine years (meaning they can continue earning a sizable amount of interest off that money), the reality is that the Sacklers will almost certainly remain one of the wealthiest families in America.[31]

To date, the Sacklers have not admitted any wrongdoing. As recently as a 2019 deposition, Kathe Sackler said of OxyContin, "It's a very good medicine, and it's a very effective and safe medicine."[32] How insensitive and out of touch with reality is this comment? While the company has twice pleaded guilty to federal crimes, the Sacklers themselves have avoided criminal charges, and the settlement will ensure they continue to do so, as it includes sweeping immunity from future opioid lawsuits.[33]

So, if you want to blame someone for addiction, blame the Sacklers. Blame Big Pharma. Blame the people who knew this drug was addictive but lied to us, told us it was safe, and pumped it into our communities.

Cannabis and opioids are very different drugs. As we'll explore in the next chapter, cannabis is far safer than many people realize. Due to the nature of cannabis, I do not believe cannabis retailers will be creating addicts the way Purdue Pharma did, but it's still important to understand this Big Lie because some of your customers may have struggled with addiction and need compassion from you.

[30] Keefe, *Empire of Pain*, 432.

[31] Hoffman, "Purdue Pharma Is Dissolved."

[32] Keefe, *Empire of Pain*, 6.

[33] Hoffman, "Purdue Pharma is Dissolved."

THE CONSEQUENCES OF THESE LIES

These Big Lies are all connected. Without racism, cannabis wouldn't have been stigmatized. Without the stigma against cannabis, we would have had a nonaddictive alternative to opioids. Without the lies that opioids are safe and that addicts are to blame for addiction, Nikki would still have her father, and hundreds of thousands more people would still be alive today.

Racism caused the Opioid Endemic. Fears of Black people, combined with lies told to us by entitled white people, who perpetrated the largest crime of this century, created this version of addiction. If you have lost a loved one to the Opioid Endemic, racism killed him or her. Among many other very human reasons, this is why racism is an issue of public health. If you're someone who thinks racism doesn't exist, I want you to really sit with this chapter for a while. Not only does racism exist, but it has been actively used as a tool against all of us—all of us who have lost loved ones to the Opioid Endemic, all of us who have suffered because of the criminalization and stigma against cannabis. Our enemy is not and never has been Black people. It's those who lie to us, who take fear and turn it against us. It's the racist white guy who perpetuated lies about Black people and cannabis to keep his job and further his personal agenda. It's the wealthy pharmaceutical family that lied to us about opioids and addiction so that they could get even richer.

I wish I could say these lies are in the past, but they remain alive and well today. When he was a US attorney in Alabama in the 1980s, former Attorney General Jeff Sessions said he thought the KKK "were okay until I found out they smoked pot." In April 2016, he said, "Good people don't smoke marijuana."[34] In 2021, Nebraska governor Pete Ricketts said, "If you

---

[34] James Higdon, "Jeff Sessions' Coming War on Legal Marijuana," Politico, December 5, 2016, https://www.politico.com/magazine/story/2016/12/jeff-sessions-coming-war-on-legal-marijuana-214501.

legalize marijuana, you're gonna kill your kids."[35] As long as these lies exist, people are going to remain uneducated and misinformed, leading to a stigma against cannabis, and that stigma has consequences.

In many instances, even in states with recreational legalization, cannabis users are still fundamentally risking their jobs and livelihoods due to the classification of cannabis as a Schedule I drug. That law controls any company that is federally regulated, like banks and insurance companies. I'm sure you've faced your own headaches trying to gain access to banking, and insurance companies hold cannabis usage against workers, charging higher rates to those companies who don't ensure "drug-free work environments." This means that many jobs still drug test, which can prevent a cannabis user from being hired, get them fired, or interfere with their workers' compensation. Do I think people should be high on the job? No. However, there are plenty of mechanisms to ingest cannabis that do not produce psychoactive effects, and I believe workers should be allowed to use cannabis however they like in their personal time. Similar rules should apply to cannabis as apply to alcohol.

I know someone who works as a supervisor for a railroad company in Mississippi. He was involved in a freak accident that resulted in his hand being mangled. He has never smoked while on the job, but he does use cannabis on his personal time, which is not surprising to me considering the physical toll of this kind of work. Per workers' comp rules on a drug-free workplace, he was drug tested, and they found cannabis in his system. It doesn't matter that he did it off the clock. His workers' compensation is now attempting to refuse to pay for his injury. Meanwhile, because it's

---

[35] William Cummings, "Nebraska Gov. Ricketts Warns: 'If You Legalize Marijuana, You're Going to Kill Your Kids," *USA Today*, March 12, 2021, https://www.usatoday.com/story/news/politics/2021/03/12/nebraska-gov-pete-ricketts-legal-marijuana-kill-your-kids/4663466001/.

Mississippi and there's no legal access to cannabis, his doctors tried to give him opioids to manage his pain.

You can't use cannabis because the government says it's addictive and has no medical use, so instead you're offered a drug that has addicted millions of people. What an ironic, vicious circle of damage. Any state that has not normalized cannabis as an alternative method of pain management is actively creating addicts today. They may not be doing it on purpose, but if the only pain medication available is opioids, addiction will be the unintended consequence. The most effective way to recover from the Opioid Endemic is to not get people addicted in the first place. This perpetuates the endemic and prolongs our collective recovery.

The stigma against cannabis has consequences for us as retailers too. Many of your customers might enter your store feeling scared or ashamed, believing falsehoods. Your community might not appreciate your presence. On a personal level, you might feel uncomfortable speaking about your job in certain situations, like around other parents or at non-industry-specific professional events.

As professionals in this industry, it's our responsibility and in our best interest to replace these Big Lies with Big Truths:

- The criminalization of cannabis is a form of institutional racism, with Black people and minorities being disproportionately impacted by the War on Drugs.
- For many people, cannabis is safe and is a legitimate alternative for pain management, as well as treatment for dozens of other medical conditions.

- Opioids are extremely addictive for some individuals, making alternatives to pain management not just important, but *necessary* to improve the collective health of our nation.
- Addiction is a disease that is not a moral failing of any one individual, and those individuals should not be treated as lepers. The best solution is to implement policies that do not create new addicts—that includes removing cannabis drug-testing policies and providing true legal access to clean, lab-tested cannabis.

When it comes to breaking the stigma, you are on the front lines. In knowing the truth about where the stigma came from and why it's so harmful, you can begin to change it. One customer at a time, you can begin to undo the Big Lies and share the reality of cannabis.

Chapter 2

THE REALITY OF CANNABIS

Today, I'm one of the biggest supporters of cannabis you'll find, but I was raised on the anticannabis messaging of the eighties and nineties. I bought into the lies that cannabis was dangerous and bad. When people talked about using cannabis for pain management, I'd roll my eyes and think, *They just want to get high.* As I became better educated and learned where these lies had come from, I began questioning all my beliefs surrounding cannabis. I wanted to get past the lies and stigma to the reality.

There's this show I love called *River Monsters.* Whenever the host, Jeremy Wade, visits a place with a potential river monster, he often starts his investigation with the myth of the creature. The reasoning is that the myth must have some semblance of truth behind it. After all, the myth had to come from somewhere. For me, the idea that cannabis could be used for pain management was a myth. I'd heard so many stories about people using cannabis for pain, or anxiety and depression, or any number of other medical reasons. For a long time, they were just that for me: stories. Then I started to think, *This many people can't be wrong.*

Later, after quitting my corporate job and transitioning to the cannabis industry, I had the opportunity to actually test that hypothesis. I was serving as the troop leader for my daughter's Girl Scout troop, and I shared with the other moms that I worked in cannabis. Slowly, one by one, they each approached me privately to ask about my work and cannabis in general. One of the moms had chronic aches and pains. She regularly got massages, went to the chiropractor, and did daily stretches to try to manage the pain. Another mom's neck was collapsing, and she was one bad car accident away from breaking her neck and dying. She had a surgery in which she had a long metal rod inserted along her spine to provide support, resulting in a scar from the nape of her neck to the middle of her back. It was a potentially life-saving procedure, but it resulted in a good deal of pain.

Both of these women came to me and essentially said, "I don't want to be high, but I have this pain. Is there anything you can do?" Around the same time, one of my dad's buddies, who was like an uncle to me, was also complaining of aches and pains. I'm personally fortunate enough not to suffer from chronic pain, but I now had three different individuals, with different kinds of pain, asking for help. I figured this was my opportunity to run my own science test on cannabis and pain management.

I found a recipe to make cannabis oil and gathered the ingredients. I then created a topical from the oil, handed it out to my "test subjects," and waited for the results. It worked, for every single one of them. As soon as they ran out, they asked for more. They didn't turn into stoners or druggies. They kept living their lives like normal, only with less pain.

It was an epiphany for me that triggered a lot of conflicting feelings.

On the one hand, I was happy that my friends were suffering less, but on the other hand, I felt sick to my stomach that Purdue Pharma had pushed opioids into our country when we had a legitimate alternative. A lot of their marketing revolved around the idea that we needed opioids because all these people were suffering from pain with no solution, but all along, we had a nonaddictive, safe solution right under our noses. It just happened to be a solution that the Sacklers couldn't monetize. My friend who had the neck surgery later confided in me that she'd previously struggled with an opioid addiction. I hate to think of what might have happened to her without cannabis to manage her pain. Either she would have suffered with her pain, or she would have risked getting addicted to opioids again.

The fact we've been told such dangerous, harmful lies about cannabis makes me deeply angry. Frankly, I'm pissed off that cannabis is categorized as a Schedule I drug. Depending on the state they live in, many people have to risk fines, jail time, or the loss of their job to use this legitimate method of pain management. Just a few years ago, my Uncle Johnny was prescribed and subsequently became addicted to opioids after a shoulder surgery. His doctor wouldn't wean him off, and he ended up having to find a rehab facility to withdraw. Though he successfully entered recovery, he still suffered from pain, which would make it even harder for him to avoid relapse. I shared my topical with him and taught my aunt how to make it, and it has been very helpful for him. However, he and his wife live in a state where cannabis remains illegal, so they could both be subject to prosecution—for something that doesn't even cause a high!

The stigma and the laws around cannabis do not reflect the reality, and they breed shame and fear. This is why it's so important for us to be educated so that we can then educate our customers and the public about the reality of cannabis, dispelling the myths, shame, and fear.

IS CANNABIS DANGEROUS?

Let's start with the big question: Is cannabis dangerous? For the most part, *no*.

Cannabis does not kill people the way other drugs do. Using too much cannabis may result in an unpleasant experience, but it will not kill you. Per the DEA, not a single death from overdose of cannabis has ever been reported.[36] Let me repeat: there have been zero overdose deaths related to cannabis usage.

Neither will stopping the use of cannabis kill you. With other drugs, including alcohol, abruptly ceasing use of the drug can lead to potentially fatal withdrawals. That is not the case with cannabis.

All of this said, almost nothing in our world is completely black and white. Some cannabis proponents act as if cannabis is a miracle drug that is 100 percent right for 100 percent of people. Remember what else was called a miracle drug? OxyContin. Part of our responsibility in doing and being better is being honest and transparent about cannabis, instead of pushing an agenda for profit. If we pretend that cannabis is perfect, we will do a disservice to our customers and our industry.

The truth is that cannabis isn't for everyone. Take me, for instance. The reason I don't use cannabis is because being high is an unpleasant experience for me. Whether it's a sativa or an indica, flower or edible, being high makes me anxious, so I don't use it.

Cannabis should also not be used recreationally among children. Regular cannabis use could have an impact on brain development, and the younger

---

[36] Drug Enforcement Administration, "Drug Fact Sheet: Marijuana/Cannabis," April 2020, https://www. dea.gov/factsheets/marijuana.

a person is when they begin using, the greater the risk for dependence or harmful use.[37] It's important that we, as a society, properly educate children on cannabis and other drugs, and that means moving away from the catch-all approach that groups drugs together and labels them all equally "bad." I run what I call "an openly narcotic-free household," where instead of hiding the existence of drugs or the nature of my job, we talk openly about different drugs and their appropriate uses. By focusing on education, my hope is that I teach my daughter to never touch an opioid, because there's no way to know her addiction potential, and to only use drugs like alcohol or cannabis in a safe manner, when she is old enough.

There may be other subsets of the population that shouldn't use cannabis, like pregnant women or people with psychotic disorders, but unfortunately, due to the Schedule I classification, the number of scientific studies on cannabis are limited. This is one more thing you can add to your list of things to be mad about.

Cannabis is not addictive in the same way that opioids and other hard drugs are, but minor addictions are possible. Particularly if a long-term, high-dose user quits, they may experience slight withdrawal symptoms, like restlessness, nervousness, irritability, loss of appetite, and difficulty sleeping.[38] Some people may use cannabis so frequently and heavily that it negatively impacts other areas of their life, which could be considered an addiction using the American Society of Addiction Medicine's definition: "People with addiction use substances or engage in behaviors that become

---

[37] Canadian Institute for Substance Use Research, "Cannabis Use and Youth: A Parent's Guide," Here to Help, accessed May 20, 2021, https://www.heretohelp.bc.ca/workbook/cannabis-use-and-youth-a-parents-guide.

[38] Canadian Institute for Substance Use Research.

compulsive and often continue despite harmful consequences."[39] However, based on the few scientific studies we have, cannabis use is less likely to lead to addiction compared to other illicit drugs, and the addiction itself is less severe.[40] According to leading experts on addiction (including Dr. Neal L. Benowitz of the University of California at San Francisco and Dr. Jack E. Henningfield of the National Institute on Drug Abuse), cannabis is also less addictive than both alcohol and tobacco, with users becoming addicted to alcohol and tobacco more quickly and experiencing a more difficult time quitting compared to cannabis.[41] It's also important to note that most people do *not* get addicted to cannabis,[42] which is a strong argument for reclassifying it, since Schedule I drugs are supposed to have "a high potential for abuse."

The method of consumption can also come with certain risks. Any kind of smoking can irritate the respiratory tract, and frequent smoking can lead to inflammation and chronic coughing or shortness of breath. However, studies suggest that the risk of developing cancer from cannabis smoking is low.[43] You can avoid the respiratory concerns with edibles, but because of the delayed onset of effects, it can be easier to take more than desired, which can lead to negative experiences.

With any drug, there are risks and benefits. I'd actually argue that the biggest risks of cannabis arise not from the substance itself but from the

---

[39] American Society of Addiction Medicine, "Definition of Addiction," accessed July 15, 2021, https://www.asam.org/Quality-Science/definition-of-addiction.

[40] Alan J. Budney, Roger Roffman, Robert S. Stephens, and Denise Walker, "Marijuana Dependence and Its Treatment," *Addiction Science and Clinical Practice* 4, no. 1 (2007): 4–16, https://www.ncbi.nlm.nih.gov/pmc/articles/PMC2797098/.

[41] Dana Tims, "Marijuana Is Less Addictive Than Both Alcohol and Tobacco," PolitiFact, June 4, 2014, https://www.politifact.com/factchecks/2014/jun/04/earl-blumenauer/marijuana-less-addictive-both-alcohol-and-tobacco/.

[42] Budney, Roffman, Stephens, and Walker, "Marijuana Dependence and Its Treatment."

[43] Canadian Institute for Substance Use Research, "Cannabis Use and Youth."

stigma. These risks include potential criminal prosecution, loss of one's job, and societal judgment. Still, for the vast majority of cannabis users, the benefits greatly outweigh the risks. Let's look more closely at those benefits, on both an individual and societal level.

Q&A with Betty Mitchell, CEO of Tively

Many people in the cannabis industry have a story about how they discovered the benefits of cannabis. Betty's story is particularly powerful to me.

Q: **How did you get started in the cannabis industry?**

A: I got my start through my uncle, Dr. Ulysses Hunter, or Uncle Ben to me. He had a PhD in physics and worked as a professor at the University of Arkansas at Pine Bluff, a historically Black university. He was absolutely brilliant, and also very compassionate. He worked on a whole other level of processing life, like no one I've ever known, then or now.

One day he came to my little small hometown to make some visits. I was immediately curious, wondering, *Where is he going?* So I went with him. He had these Mason jars in the back of his car, and he drove around delivering them to people. Come to find out, he'd created a cannabis-based pain medicine. Cannabis isn't naturally water soluble, but he worked out a recipe using a natural excipient he created that made it much more water soluble, so he was able to create an edible that you could consume directly, add to food or drinks, or cook with.

At that time—in the sixties and early seventies—we had migrant workers who would come through Arkansas, and you still had Black folks out there chopping cotton and picking beans, if you can believe it. I watched my parents pick cotton in the sixties, and talk about hard labor. I'm sixty-one, and when my parents were my age, they looked like they were eighty years old. That work was hard on the body. Injuries were common—broken arms, cracked ribs, snakebites, fractures. But folks didn't have health insurance. You could go to some kind of hospital or clinic to get splints and the like, but when it came to pain management, people went to my uncle. He was our local healer.

I was so impressed with him and what he was doing for our community, and I became enthralled. He was secretive about it, because he had to be. He never disclosed where he grew the cannabis or processed it. But as the years went on, he was very forthcoming with me. I became his student, and before he passed, he gave me his recipe. Today, I'm now using an improved version of his formula and carrying on the tradition.

Q: Why is your work in cannabis important?

A: My uncle knew—he knew—that cannabis had medicinal properties. He told me in 1975, "They will use this like medicine someday." Sure enough, that's what people are trying to do today, because it works.

For me, the epiphany moment came when I had two good friends with terminal cancer. Seeing them in pain, I thought, *You know what? I got a formula that can help with that.* I got some cannabis, contracted with an FDA laboratory to create the excipient base, and blended up my uncle's formula. Then another friend and I cooked up soft cookies with it, and on a Sunday afternoon, we took them over to our friend, who had transitioned into hospice, with just a few weeks to live.

I'll never forget it. I'd read about the medicinal benefits of cannabis a thousand times, but this was my first time really seeing what it could do. My friend was propped up in her bed, very weak, barely talking. She had difficulty swallowing, so we fed her slowly—little bit of cookie, little bit of water, little cookie, little water. Thirty, forty minutes in, she was sitting up straighter, and she was talking. She had such a sense of humor, and she started joking about how she should've killed her ex-husband 'cause she's dying. We thought, *Oh my God, did we give her too much?* But seriously, within an hour and a half, you should have seen the transformation. She talked about her years running a day care, her kids, her thoughts about her cancer. It was the most she'd spoken in weeks. Cannabis eased her pain, allowed me to leave nothing unsaid, and it gave me another beautiful memory of my friend.

My other friend with cancer—metastatic stage III going into stage IV— transitioned from this world at her home. The cancer had moved all through her body, causing a lot of pain. She'd been given a lot of prescription pain management, and I discovered that a relative had been stealing her medicine. We went to see her to give her some cookies as well, and I saw her whole energy field literally change. She was out of pain, talking and joking. And she was cognizant. When so many people think of cannabis, they think you sit there and smoke all day in a sluggish haze. It wasn't like that.

These experiences were enough to make me want to spend $300,000 to get my company going. Our healthcare system is broken in many ways. I'm a social worker, and I know plenty of people who don't have any real health insurance. If you've never had to pay full price for medication, consider yourself fortunate. It's outrageously expensive. Even people who do have health insurance can't always afford their copays. So cannabis is important not just because it's effective, but because it's affordable. I can create a canna-bis cookie for just twenty-five cents, and it's all natural and not addictive. That inspires me.

I also think it's unfortunate that they didn't start earlier using cannabis as a psychotropic drug to manage bipolar disorder and other mental illnesses. I think of all the people we've lost to suicide and how cannabis might have changed that. I also think of all those who've died from overdoses. I've lost two of my students to prescription pain medicine overdoses. One of them was within the past year, and she had been doing so well, going to school, working. Then she took a fifteen-dollar pill laced with fentanyl, and she died in her sleep at only twenty-one years old. I knew she suffered from long-standing depression; I wish she'd spoken to me or had access to cannabis instead. Even twenty, thirty years ago, had cannabis been legal, I don't think we would have had the alcoholism and crack use that took Black folks out. So absolutely, our work in cannabis is important.

MEDICAL BENEFITS

Schedule I drugs are supposed to have "no currently accepted medical use," but cannabis has many medical benefits, which is the other half of the argument for why it needs to be reclassified.

The most common medical use of cannabis is pain management. Cannabis does not take pain down to zero like opioids do, but it makes the pain more manageable. If, for example, your pain is an 8 on a 0–10 scale, cannabis might take it down to a 3. In many cases, that's preferable. Pain is meant to be a warning system that something's wrong. Say I break my toe, and I take something that completely eliminates the pain. Now I might decide to go dancing, because I feel great. Then I wake up tomorrow and discover I've done more damage to my toe without realizing it because I couldn't feel any pain. With cannabis, enough of the warning system remains intact to keep you aware of what's happening with your body.

Cannabis has a number of other uses beyond pain management. It can help with nausea, loss of appetite, and weight loss (either due to eating disorders or an underlying disease). Many people also use cannabis to manage the symptoms of mental health conditions, like anxiety, depression, and PTSD. While qualifying medical conditions vary by state, these are some of the conditions for which cannabis is frequently prescribed:[44]

- Cancer (particularly to treat the side effects of chemotherapy)
- Epilepsy and seizures
- Multiple sclerosis and muscle spasms
- Alzheimer's disease
- Amyotrophic lateral sclerosis (ALS)
- HIV/AIDS
- Crohn's disease
- Glaucoma

Frankly, we don't yet know the full medical potential of cannabis because the Schedule I classification creates many barriers for scientific studies. As a consensus study report from the National Academies of Sciences, Engineering, and Medicine states:

---

[44] "Medical Marijuana," Mayo Clinic, November 27, 2019, https://www.mayoclinic.org/healthy-lifestyle /consumer-health/in-depth/medical-marijuana/art-20137855.

The federal government has not legalized cannabis and continues to enforce restrictive policies and regulations on research into the health harms or benefits of cannabis products that are available to consumers in a majority of states. As a result, research on the health effects of cannabis and cannabinoids has been limited in the United States, leaving patients, health care professionals, and policymakers without the evidence they need to make sound decisions regarding the use of cannabis and cannabinoids. This lack of evidence-based information on the health effects of cannabis and cannabinoids poses a public health risk.[45]

While more research is needed, the consensus study report found substantial and conclusive evidence that cannabis is a legitimate medicine for multiple conditions.[46]

Lobbying Against Cannabis: Where Does the Money Come From?

When it comes to the legalization of cannabis, a lot of money has been spent lobbying on both sides of the issue. In most instances, lobbying reports do not identify the specific issues a lobbying entity supports or opposes, but the Center for Responsive Politics (a nonpartisan, independent nonprofit)

---

[45] National Academies of Sciences, Engineering, and Medicine, "Challenges and Barriers in Conducting Cannabis Research," in *The Health Effects of Cannabis and Cannabinoids: The Current State of Evidence and Recommendations for Research* (Washington, DC: National Academies Press, 2017), https://www.ncbi.nlm.nih.gov/books/NBK425757/.

[46] National Academies of Sciences, Engineering, and Medicine, "Therapeutic Effects of Cannabis and Cannabinoids," in *The Health Effects of Cannabis and Cannabinoids: The Current State of Evidence and Recommendations for Research* (Washington, DC: National Academies Press, 2017), https://www.ncbi.nlm.nih.gov/books/NBK425767/.

has identified the following interest groups that have reason to oppose cannabis legalization: [47]

- **Pharmaceutical corporations.** Because cannabis offers an alternative to traditional medicines, pharmaceutical companies have a vested interest in keeping it illegal. When cannabis legalization was on the ballot in Arizona, for instance, the pharmaceutical company Insys Therapeutics (which produces a fentanyl-derived painkiller) was the largest donor to the antilegalization campaign, with a $500,000 contribution.[48] Additionally, Purdue Pharma (maker of OxyContin) and Abbott Laboratories (maker of Vicodin) are two of the largest contributors to the Anti-Drug Coalition of America, and in 2015 alone, the Pharmaceutical Research and Manufacturers of America, which is believed to be one of the biggest opponents of legalized cannabis, spent nearly $19 million on lobbying.[49]

- **Private prisons.** To remain profitable, private prisons need inmates, and nonviolent drug offenses are a great (or terrible, depending on how you look at it) way to fill beds. According to the Center for Responsive Politics, "Since 2008, the Corrections Corporation of America has spent at least $970,000 a year on lobbying."[50] While they claim to not lobby for or against policies that would affect whether someone is incarcerated, I personally wonder what all that money is for.

---

[47] Brianna Gurciullo, "The Money in Marijuana: The Political Landscape," Center for Responsive Politics, last updated November 2015, https://www.opensecrets.org/news/issues/marijuana/.

[48] Alfonso Serrano, "Inside Big Pharma's Fight to Block Recreational Marijuana," *Guardian*, October 22, 2016, https://www.theguardian.com/sustainable-business/2016/oct/22/recreational-marijuana-legalization-big-business.

[49] Ibid.

[50] Gurciullo, "The Money in Marijuana."

- **Alcohol industry.** Cannabis could potentially be a competitor for alcohol, so the alcohol industry may wish to oppose its legalization. In Arizona, the Arizona Wine and Spirits Wholesale Association donated $10,000 to antilegalization efforts, and in Massachusetts, the Beer Distributors PAC donated $25,000 to the Campaign for a Safe and Healthy Massachusetts (another antilegalization organization).[51]
- **Police and prison guard unions.** The War on Drugs generates a lot of revenue, both from government funding and from the property seized during drug raids. As such, police and prison guard unions have reasons to see cannabis remain illegal. Combined, various police union organizations spend about $540,000 a year in lobbying, and many prison guards are represented by the American Federation of State, County and Municipal Employees, which spent $11 million during the 2014 election cycle and an additional $2.4 million on lobbying in 2014.[52]

While many of the antilegalization efforts we see stem from people who legitimately, though wrongly, believe that cannabis is dangerous, it's important to recognize that a lot of the campaigning likely arises from self-serving interests.

ECONOMIC BENEFITS

The cannabis industry generates a *lot* of revenue and is undergoing rapid growth. In the United States in 2020, the medical cannabis industry produced

---

[51] Serrano, "Inside Big Pharma's Fight."

[52] Gurciullo, "The Money in Marijuana."

$7.3 billion in sales, and recreational produced $10.2 billion, representing a 40 percent increase year over year.[53] By 2026, the total market is expected to grow to $41.2 billion ($9.9 medical, $31.3 recreational).[54]

One of the best parts? That money stays in the United States. That's the one good thing about cannabis being a Schedule I drug. In so many other industries, including farming and agriculture, work is outsourced, and products are imported. Not only does that hurt American companies and employees, but it can lead to systems of exploitation. When (and I do believe it's *when*, not *if*) cannabis is legalized federally, it will be critical that regulations include provisions to keep the cultivation, manufacturing, and retail of cannabis domestic.

Because the cannabis industry legally cannot be outsourced, it creates many US jobs. In 2020, when many industries were stagnating or declining due to the COVID-19 pandemic, the cannabis industry created more than 77,000 jobs, for a total of 321,000 full-time American jobs across the legal cannabis industry.[55] Plus, these jobs tend to be good, well-paying positions, with no college degree needed. California, as one of the most mature markets of cannabis retail, has set many of the standards of the industry, including the standard of paying workers a living wage as opposed to minimum wage. Additionally, because licensing is so competitive and often merit-based, those retailers that agree to pay a living wage are more likely to secure licenses. With a living wage standard, cannabis employment can be not just a job, but a legitimate *career*.

---

[53] Kelly Nielsen, "Winning In-Store: Upsell, Cross-Sell, and a Prediction of this Year's 4/20," BDSA, webinar, March 31, 2021, https://resources.bdsa.com/winning-in-store-recording.

[54] Ibid.

[55] Bruce Barcott, Beau Whitney, and Janessa Bailey, *Leafly Jobs Report 2021*, Leafly, February 16, 2021, https://www.leafly.com/news/industry/cannabis-jobs-report.

Beyond creating jobs within the industry (in cultivation, manufacturing, and retail), the cannabis industry triggers job creation and economic growth in surrounding industries. When a city invites a cannabis business into the community, that business will need to retrofit and renovate a facility to suit its needs—tearing down and adding walls, installing lighting and flooring, updating plumbing, and so on. That means hiring contractors or tradespeople, who will almost always be local and buy their supplies locally as well. Once the business is up and running, the employees, who are making a living wage, will continue to pump money back into the community, spending their salaries at restaurants, grocery stores, and other local businesses. In addition to these economic ripple effects, the legalization of cannabis would likely mean the elimination of pre-employment drug testing for cannabis, which would increase applicant pools for many companies, which is good for business. In fact, in 2021, Amazon made the decision to stop testing for cannabis and to support cannabis legalization for this reason, additionally citing the fact that such testing disproportionately impacts people of color.[56] Considering Amazon is one of the US's largest employers, this is likely to set precedent for other employers to follow suit.

Because cannabis is such a high-value crop, the economic potential is huge and can cascade down to all levels of the industry. Basically, there's enough money for *everyone* involved in cannabis, not just the players at the top, and that's the kind of industry our country needs more of.

---

[56] Beth Galetti, "Amazon Is Supporting the Effort to Reform the Nation's Cannabis Policy," Amazon, September 21, 2021, https://www.aboutamazon.com/news/policy-news-views/amazon-is-supporting -the-effort-to-reform-the-nations-cannabis-policy.

Social Equity Done Right

Through social equity programs, the cannabis industry has the opportunity to help right some of the racist wrongs of the past. Unfortunately, while most states have adopted social equity programs, and their hearts are in the right place, few of these programs are truly effective. Across the industry, only 1.2 to 1.7 percent of all cannabis company owners are Black (for context, Black Americans make up about 13 percent of the population).[57]

The biggest barrier that is not accounted for in most current social equity programs is access to capital. Because cannabis is federally illegal, securing bank loans is next to impossible, which means start-up capital must come from personal wealth. Per a 2019 survey, while the median family wealth for white Americans is $188,200, it is only $24,100 for Black Americans.[58] Many Black entrepreneurs who would like to enter the cannabis space simply cannot afford to. Even when cannabis is federally legalized, Black Americans will still face greater difficulties securing capital due to discrimination in banking. Recent data from the US Federal Reserve shows that more than half of companies with Black owners were turned down for loans—a rate of double their white counterparts.[59] Some private groups and individuals have stepped up to help address this disparity—Jay-Z, for instance, created a $10 million fund for minority-owned cannabis businesses[60]—but more needs to be done.

[57] Barcott, Whitney, and Bailey, *Leafly Jobs Report 2021*.

[58] Neil Bhutta, Andrew C. Chang, Lisa J. Dettling, and Joanne W. Hsu, "Disparities in Wealth by Race and Ethnicity in the 2019 Survey of Consumer Finances," FEDS Notes, Washington: Board of Governors of the Federal Reserve System, September 28, 2020, https://doi.org/10.17016/2380-7172.2797.

[59] Gene Marks, "Black-Owned Firms Are Twice as Likely to Be Rejected for Loans. Is This Discrimination?," *Guardian*, January 16, 2020, https://www.theguardian.com/business/2020/jan/16/black-owned-firms-are-twice-as-likely-to-be-rejected-for-loans-is-this-discrimination.

[60] Barcott, Whitney, and Bailey, *Leafly Jobs Report 2021*.

Another important barrier to be considered is education. I've helped many retailers secure their cannabis licenses, and as I'm sure you know, it's a Herculean task. Form after form, filled with legalese, and if you make even one mistake, you'll get rejected. The competition is that intense. If you don't have a legal background or the money to hire someone like me to help, you're at a significant disadvantage. Then, once you actually begin running your store, you'll face many more challenges. If you don't have access to the right education and resources, which many Black Americans don't, it can be difficult to succeed.

The best social equity program I've seen, the Cannabis Opportunity Reinvestment and Equity (CORE) Program in Sacramento, California, addresses these two barriers. It's a tuition-free program that teaches participants how to succeed in the cannabis trade. Part of the program is CORE Capital, a six-year, interest-free loan program, which provides a series of loans up to a total of $125,000. While this isn't enough to fully open a store, it's a huge help. This kind of program is the direction we need to move in.

What legislators can do to improve social equity as related to cannabis:

- **Don't overly limit the number of licenses.** The fewer licenses you give out, the more you're encouraging people to game the system, with white business owners taking steps to qualify for social equity.
- **Help minority business owners access start-up capital.** It takes more than a license to open a cannabis business; it takes money, and a lot of it.
- **Provide education and assistance.** This sets minority owners up for success both in the license application process and the running of their business.

- **Interview applicants in person.** This way, you can ensure licenses are being distributed on true merit and not on gamesmanship of the system.

What we as retailers can do:

Form real partnerships with minority entrepreneurs. These partnerships can be invaluable to both parties. I've set many of these partnerships up myself, but I make it very clear that I will not tolerate bad behavior on the part of the financial partner. I've unfortunately heard of some retailers using their minority "partner" to take advantage of social equity programs. Then, once they've secured their license, they slowly push the minority partner out of the picture, not paying them the salary they deserve as the business grows. We're better than that. Don't become a partner unless you're going to act like it.

Adopt diversity and inclusion policies in hiring, and create paths for advancement to leadership positions. We don't just need minority owners in the cannabis industry; we need minority leaders too.

Share your knowledge. If you've gone through the licensing process and have been operating a store for a while, you have a lot of great knowledge and experience you can share. Spending a few hours of your time to pass this on or becoming a long-term mentor to a minority entrepreneur can make a huge difference.

Q&A with Betty Mitchell, CEO of Tively

As a minority owner and the first graduate of the Sacramento CORE program, Betty has a valuable perspective on social equity in the cannabis industry as well as helpful advice for cannabis retailers.

Q: **What challenges did you face starting your company?**

A: When Prop 64 [to legalize cannabis in California] was on the ballot, I stayed up the whole night to see if it passed, and it did. Literally the next day, I was outlining my business plan. Every night, until the early hours of the morning, I was working. That's how much I wanted to do this. I was one of the very first submittals for the city of Sacramento. With anything, the first ones through the doors get the bloodiest. I faced massive, massive challenges. Nobody was really ready to handle cannabis ventures—the city, the building department, even the engineers—so getting my warehouse built was difficult. After spending $16,800 on a CUP [conditional use permit] application and around $30,000 on a floor plan designed for a specific warehouse I had leased, and $9,800 for the BOP [business operating permit], the owners sold the building out from under me. All that money I'd invested was just gone, zeroed out. It was a huge blow, but fighting it would have cost thousands more in legal fees, and it would have taken months, maybe years. Either I could stop everything and fight this battle, or I could move forward with the money I still had and try to find another location. I chose the latter. I got a hold of a broker, and he was incredible. He found me a much better building, with a wonderful landlord and a much better lease agreement. He saved me from bankruptcy.

Q: What did you get out of the Sacramento CORE program?

A: The CORE program was manna. It was great. I'd gone to a lot of paid seminars and studied profusely—and learned a lot through trial and error—so I personally knew a lot of the information already. But the very first night, I thought, *This program can work*, because the instructor shared a lot of the missteps that I myself had made. I knew exactly how valuable the information was, and I was also able to share my own experiences with the other folks. The program brought in engineers, lawyers, and accountants— all things I didn't have access to at all.

The program also gave us networking opportunities and the chance to build a community. I'm still very active in the CORE program. Always, if someone needs help or advice, I'm there. I've helped write business plans, done building walkthroughs before lease signings, given input on branding, and I do it all free of charge, because I know how arduous this process is. I tell people, "I don't do favors. You owe me nothing. The only thing I want you to do is follow through." I'm so proud of what I've seen people accomplish. And I hope that they'll pay it forward. I never want to find out that someone I helped later refused to help someone else.

Q: What would make social equity programs more effective?

A: They need to provide access to money. Money is the barrier. Education and networking opportunities are helpful, but without money, you can't get a business started. This is a big reason why most of the people who've been successful in the cannabis space are middle-aged white men or women, because they're the ones who have the money to do it. A small vendor like me, who had to cash out my annuities to get started, is competing against people with a $5 million starting budget. All the rules are the same for us, and we have to pay the same costs, but we have vastly different budgets. That's what makes the cannabis industry unfair.

Some social equity programs do give out money, but they make the mistake of giving out too little. I've seen programs give out $25,000, which is nothing when it comes to opening a cannabis business. Minimum, I think programs should give out $100,000, and they should make it receipts-based, where the entrepreneur spends their own money and then gets reimbursed after submitting the receipts. That will prevent people from wasting the money, and it ensures they're really invested because they're spending their own money first.

If you want to start a nonstorefront or a small manufacturing company with $100,000 of your own money and $100,000 from social equity, you can get in the game. For storefront and cultivation businesses, you need even more, but $100,000 can still have a real impact, where $25,000 doesn't.

Q: What advice would you give to minority entrepreneurs?

A: First, you need money in the bank, at least $100,000, liquid and ready to go. I've worked with several people who had outstanding potential, but because they didn't have the funds, they couldn't get their businesses off the ground. Don't kid yourself with relatives or friends who promise to invest a certain amount. Until that money is actually in your account, you can't count on it. You can't count on loans or lines of credit either, at least at first. Once you're up and running, you may get more access to those things because you've already proven you have what it takes to survive and people will see you as a smart risk.

Second, you can't be scared to be in this thing. I won't sugarcoat it: it's tough, and it ain't for everybody. You're going to have to work *hard*. Even if you go through a course like Sacramento's CORE program, it's not going to put you in business. There's a whole lot more you need to do. You have to be ready to work, but if you're scared and start making your decisions out of fear, you're not going to make it. You need a high tolerance for uncertainty.

Third, get a lawyer involved from the beginning, especially if you have partners. Yes, lawyers can be expensive, but it's difficult to keep deals together, and you can get really hurt down the line if you don't protect yourself. I never learned how to play well in the sandbox, so I don't do partnerships. My friends and relatives swear I ruled an African dynasty in my last life.

Finally, you have to learn to work with white people. As people of color, we don't always like to acknowledge it, but deep inside, a lot of us have a fear or distrust of white people. There's this feeling of "If I build it, they'll take it." This pathology is deep, deep in there, ingrained by decades of history, and it's reinforced today when we see Black people choked out and killed by police officers on national television. As difficult as it is, though, you have to surrender all of that at the door, or you will not get through this process or life. The simple fact is that 80 percent of people you interface with in this whole process or life are going to be white folks. It will never be a level playing field; the trick is not to let anyone get in your way.

Q: What can retailers do in terms of social equity?

A: Give minority cultivators and manufacturers shelf space. Let us be vendors, and feature our products. That's how you can help us out. Our job is to create quality products, but we need a retail platform for them.

SOCIETAL BENEFITS

The cannabis industry is not only good for cannabis users and businesses, but it is also good for society as a whole.

First, all the economic benefits of the industry help to uplift communities. Every community needs jobs for its citizens, and when people are earning a living wage, they can afford housing and begin to build generational wealth, instead of living paycheck to paycheck. Good, well-paying jobs that don't require a college education could be particularly important for small, more rural communities. Poverty and lack of opportunity have been associated with spikes in substance abuse, so these communities are often the ones hit particularly hard by the Opioid Endemic. Providing good jobs is one more way we can help combat the Opioid Endemic.

Of course, you can't forget taxes. Recreational cannabis is taxed at high rates—often in the 20 to 35 percent range. For a billion-dollar industry, that generates a ton of money, which is very often used to directly help a state's citizens. In Washington, for example, the majority of cannabis tax revenue (projected to be $1 billion for the two-year 2021–23 budget cycle) is used to provide healthcare for low-income individuals and those who lack health insurance, and some of the money funds education and substance abuse programs.[61] In Aurora, Colorado, the city used $1.5 million of its cannabis tax revenue to help combat homelessness.[62] Whatever a particular city or state needs, cannabis can help fund it.

Access to legal cannabis could also lead to a decline in opioid use and binge drinking. One study found that states with medical cannabis laws had significantly fewer opioid prescriptions in the Medicare Part D population compared to states without such laws,[63] and another study that looked at the Medicaid population found that states that had also legalized recreational use saw additional reductions in opioid prescriptions.[64] (This latter finding is not surprising to me, as in my experience, many "recreational" users are in fact self-medicating.) A different 2014 study found that states with medical cannabis laws had a 24.8 percent lower opioid overdose mortality rate compared to those without legal access to medical cannabis.[65] Similarly, a Cowen study found that people in states with recreational cannabis binge drink 13 percent fewer times per month compared to states where cannabis

[61] Melissa Santos, "How $1 Billion in Pot Taxes Gets Spent in Washington State," Crosscut, February 22, 2021, https://crosscut.com/news/2021/02/how-1-billion-pot-taxes-gets-spent-washington-state.

[62] Vice staff, "A Colorado City Is Using Tax Money from Weed to Help the Homeless," Vice, May 13, 2016, https://www.vice.com/en/article/yvxaww/a-colorado-city-is-using-tax-money-from-weed-to-help-the -homeless-vgtrn.

[63] Ashley C. Bradford et al., "Association Between US State Medical Cannabis Laws and Opioid Prescribing in the Medicare Part D Population," *JAMA Internal Medicine* 178, no. 5 (2018): 667–72, https://doi.org/10.1001/jamainternmed.2018.0266.

[64] Hefei Wen and Jason M Hockenberry, "Association of Medical and Adult-Use Marijuana Laws with Opioid Prescribing for Medicaid Enrollees," *JAMA Internal Medicine* 178, no. 5 (2018): 673–79, https://doi.org/10.1001/jamainternmed.2018.1007.

[65] Marcus A. Bachhuber et al., "Medical Cannabis Laws and Opioid Analgesic Overdose Mortality in the United States, 1999–2010," *JAMA Internal Medicine* 174, no. 10 (2014): 1668–73, https://doi.org /10.1001/jamainternmed.2014.4005.

remains illegal.[66] Fewer people binge drinking and fewer people becoming addicted to and dying from opioids is certainly a positive societal change.

Opponents of cannabis argue that legalization will lead to increased crime, more traffic accidents, and a decline in public health. In reality, studies show that legalization has not had a substantial impact on either crime rates or traffic accidents and fatalities.[67] Hopefully, in legalizing and regulating the industry, we can actually lower crime associated with the illegal drug trade. Additionally, the sad reality today is that not everyone has health insurance or can afford healthcare. For these subsets of the population, medical cannabis offers a more affordable alternative, which can help to improve public health.

While many people think of cannabis as "the devil's lettuce," sure to corrupt our children and lead to the downfall of our society, the exact opposite is true. Cannabis benefits not just users and industry professionals, but society as a whole.

A LEGITIMATE MEDICINE, A LEGITIMATE INDUSTRY, AND LEGITIMATE BENEFITS FOR SOCIETY

It's easy for people unfamiliar with cannabis to dismiss it as just a drug, good only for getting high. The reality is that cannabis has many benefits. It provides an alternative to opioids for pain management and can help

---

[66] Vivien Azer, Brian Nicholas Velez, and Gerald Pascarelli, "Cannabis: $75B Opportunity; Category Cross-Currents Keep Us Cautious On Booze," Cowen, April 11, 2018, https://www.cowen.com/insights/cannabis-75b-opportunity-category-cross-currents-keep-us-cautious-on-booze/.

[67] Greg Rosalsky, "The Data On Legalizing Weed," *Planet Money*, newsletter, March 16, 2021, https://www.npr.org/sections/money/2021/03/16/976265525/the-data-on-legalizing-weed.

treat many other ailments, both physical and mental, no health insurance required. It's an economic driver that provides well-paying jobs that don't require a college education. Better public health and better economies are good for society as a whole, and cannabis has the added benefit of offering an alternative to other, more dangerous drug usage.

The cannabis industry is poised to be a major contributor to the betterment of society. The more we can do as retailers to give back and become valuable members of our communities, the more we can make the public—and legislators—see that cannabis is a legitimate medicine and a legitimate industry, with legitimate benefits for society. But in order to change people's minds about cannabis, we have to show them our legitimacy by creating a customer experience that reflects the reality of cannabis.

Chapter 3

THE CUSTOMER EXPERIENCE

I n summer 2020, my partner, Darrell, and I took our daughter and one of her friends on a thirty-day RV trip around the country, concentrated in the Southwest. When we entered Texas, we saw a billboard that made us laugh: "Only 262 miles to Bucc-ee's. You can hold it." As we kept driving, we saw more billboards, counting down the miles to the Bucc-ee's.

When we finally reached the Bucc-ee's, of course we had to stop. Never have I seen so many gas pumps in one spot—*dozens*, easily more than forty. Because there were so many pumps, we didn't have to wait in line to fuel up. As an added bonus, they were well lit and spacious, with a layout that made it easy to pull the RV in and refuel. If you've ever driven an RV, you know how delightful it is when you don't have to worry about scraping the roof or making a white-knuckle-inducing tight turn.

Like most families on vacation, as Darrell filled up the RV, the first stop for the rest of us was the bathroom. Just like the pumps, the bathroom was clean, spacious, and well lit. In most bathrooms, after you wash your hands, you then have to open the door, which defeats the purpose of washing your hands. Customers have adopted all kinds of creative methods to get around this issue—the foot prop, the paper towel mitt, the postdoor hand sanitizer. This was in the middle of the COVID-19 pandemic, so we were all much more conscious about that kind of thing. Fortunately, Bucc-ee's was one step ahead. There was no main door into the bathroom area, and everything was no touch—the water, the soap, the paper towel dispenser and hand dryer. The timing on each step was perfect too—you got the exact right amount of soap, water, and paper towel that you needed.

We then spent some time exploring the store. They had cheap ice, which we always needed, a lot of interesting souvenirs, and good food. We were in Texas, which is known for BBQ, so I got a brisket taco. It. Was. Phenomenal. I never knew I needed a brisket taco, until Bucc-ee's had one for me. We literally spent hours walking around that gas station. Even our dogs loved it because there was a special grassy area for them to do their business. Bucc-ee's had thought of absolutely everything a family might need or want while traveling, and so the entire experience was delightful.

Eventually, we headed on our way again, but we kept talking about Bucc-ee's. It became a running joke. We made our way up to Yellowstone and then started back to Florida. When we went through Texas again, you can bet we stopped at a Bucc-ee's at the first opportunity. Once again, we had a great time, and even bought some Bucc-ee's-branded souvenirs.

On that trip, we saw some of the most beautiful sights our country has to offer—the vastness of the Grand Canyon, the beautiful colors and cliffs of Zion National Park, the mountains and geysers of Yellowstone. When I think about the best, most memorable moments of the vacation, right up there with the natural splendor of the rugged Southwest, is Bucc-ee's. *That* is the power of a great customer experience.

WHY THE CUSTOMER EXPERIENCE MATTERS

Do you want to expand your customer base?

Build customer loyalty?

Improve revenue?

Stand out from the competition?

The customer experience is how you do all of that. The customer experience is *everything*, and I'm only exaggerating a little. The customer experience encompasses every single interaction your customer has with your store—from advertising and branding, to the physical store location itself, to the purchase process, to the use of your products. Anything that affects the way the customer thinks or feels about your store is part of the customer experience.

Customers—and your ability to attract and retain them—will make or break your business. A business literally cannot exist without customers. Customers are how we make a profit, and if we want customers to choose to spend their hard-earned dollars with us instead of a competitor, we need to give them a good reason to do so. We need to create a delightful customer experience, so that they enjoy shopping with us. As Maya Angelou, one of my favorite poets and people of all time, said, "People will forget what you said, people will forget what you did, but people will never forget how you made them feel."[68] With the right customer experience, we can tap into our customers' emotions so that they never forget us.

A delightful customer experience generates the most important competitive advantage you can have in this industry: customer loyalty. We are all selling the same product. While the exact selection will vary from store to store, a customer can essentially walk into any dispensary and find what they want. By default then, most customers are going to go to whichever store is most convenient for them or has the lowest prices. Theoretically, we could slash our profit margins in order to offer the cheapest prices, but that is not particularly sustainable or profitable. Rather than trying to win individual sales in this way, we should be trying to win *customers*. A single sale might be worth $100, but if you can win a customer for life, you're looking at thousands of dollars in customer lifetime value.

Not only do loyal customers generate more profit long term, but they are one of the best ways to attract new customers. I tell everyone about Bucc-ee's. If someone tells me they're going to Texas, the first thing I say is "You have to go to Bucc-ee's!" That kind of word-of-mouth advertising is hugely valuable, particularly in an industry like cannabis. Because of the stigma and the fear and shame, many customers are going to feel nervous walking into a dispensary, especially for the first time. The recommendation of someone they know and trust will have a big influence.

Finally, the customer experience is how we can begin changing the stigma. A customer might start out being afraid of cannabis or expecting us to be "lazy stoners." Through the customer experience, we can eliminate their fears and educate them, making them feel safe and comfortable. With

---

[68] Elizabeth Dori Tunstall, "How Maya Angelou Made Me Feel," The Conversation, May 29, 2014, https://theconversation.com/how-maya-angelou-made-me-feel-27328.

warm service and professional operations, we can change their image of cannabis.

THE STATE OF THE CUSTOMER EXPERIENCE IN THE CANNABIS INDUSTRY

In nearly every other retail industry, the customer experience is already front and center. In cannabis, however, the customer experience has largely been pushed to the back burner, and not without reason. After deciding to enter the cannabis space, you have to work for years—without profit—just to get to your store's grand opening. Then, in the first months and even years of operation, immediately after you put out one fire, a new one spontaneously erupts. Simply keeping your doors open and your shelves stocked with product takes all your time and energy. You can't afford to take your eye off the short-term problems and think about your long-term customer experience.

On top of that, everything in this space is new. We don't have clear role models within the industry. There's no collective history or knowledge we can look to for best retail practices. If you go to a major cannabis conference, all the speakers, booths, and events will be centered around cultivation, manufacturing, and the science behind cannabis. The innovations and new research in those spaces are, of course, important and will help drive our industry forward, but the customer experience is just as—if not more—important, because the customer experience is the medium through which cultivation and scientific discoveries can be leveraged. Put another way, you could have the *best* strain of cannabis possible, but if you have a crappy customer experience, no one's going to buy it!

Because we don't have the benefit of history or established best practices, there's not much consistency of customer experience across the industry. This is both good and bad news. The good news is that if you do take the time and energy to create a great customer experience, it'll be easy to stand out from the competition. The bad news is that bad actors and poor customer experiences reflect negatively on the industry as a whole.

I remember the very first cannabis conference I went to. I was *so* excited to learn more and form relationships with my peers in the industry. One booth ended up standing out to me, and not in a good way. The company's marketing strategy was immediately very apparent and could be boiled down to one word: sex. It was like the Hooters of the cannabis world, with several young women in tight booty shorts and bikini tops. The booth wasn't unpopular, but it immediately made me uncomfortable, and I chose to steer clear. I can guarantee that many other people made the same decision. I'd classify that as a bad customer experience because it needlessly alienated and turned off a large portion of their potential customer base. Additionally, with so many people already prejudiced against our industry, that kind of branding and messaging isn't doing us any favors.

The fact of the matter is that our industry was born of illegal operations. We can argue that cannabis shouldn't have been made illegal in the first place, but we can't change the past. Black market operators are the founding fathers of our industry, and we owe them a great deal. If they hadn't chosen to break the law and risk the consequences in order to still grow and sell cannabis, people wouldn't have been able to use cannabis and learn of its benefits. Without access to cannabis, public opinion likely wouldn't have shifted in the way it has today, and our industry very well may not exist. At the same time, those black market operators also contributed to the stigma of cannabis operators as "criminals." Still today, bad actors in the industry can give us all a bad reputation. Because of that baggage, we must adhere to a higher standard of business etiquette and professionalism within our customer experience in order to protect our integrity and overcome the stereotypes.

WHO ARE OUR CUSTOMERS?

A delightful customer experience is about anticipating and fulfilling the customer's needs and wants. To do that, you must first understand *who* your customer is.

The prevailing stereotype of a cannabis user, in large part due to media portrayals (think *Pineapple Express* and *Dude, Where's My Car?*), is the "stoner": typically male, in his twenties or thirties, lazy (or at least not ambitious), most likely to spend his time playing video games or watching movies and eating junk food. This is probably exactly the audience that cannabis booth with the half-naked women was attempting to target. Yes, some of our customers will fit this profile, but it's only one subsection of a much larger customer base. BDSA, one of the top analytics companies in the cannabis space, found that in fully legal states (with both medical and recreational cannabis legalization), *72 percent* of adults are "bought in" to consuming, with 43 percent being consumers and 29 percent being "acceptors," which means they are not currently consumers but are open to it.[69] So who are our customers? Pretty much everyone.

The cannabis user is the military veteran struggling with PTSD who uses cannabis to sleep without nightmares and dull their anxiety.

---

[69] Nielsen, "Winning In-Store."

It's the grandmother with arthritis who just wants to be able to knit again.

It's the corporate business leader who wants to unwind after a stressful week.

It's the college student who smokes socially with friends.

It's the patient with chronic pain who is looking to take the edge off.

It's the mom or dad that uses it for self-care and me time away from the kids.

There is no one single cannabis user. All sorts of different people use cannabis, for different reasons. Our job as retailers is to create stores and customer experiences that serve our diverse customer base.

CREATING A BETTER CUSTOMER EXPERIENCE

We now have the foundation set. We've explored the stigmas about and around cannabis, the reality of cannabis, and why the customer experience is so important, both in eliminating the stigma and succeeding as businesses. In Part II, we will delve into all the various aspects of the customer experience in detail:

- Leadership
- Branding
- Service
- Merchandising
- Omnichannel
- Marketing (promotions and loyalty programs in particular)
- Store operations

Each of these topics could easily be an entire book on its own, so my goal is not to provide an exhaustive, encyclopedic level of instruction. Rather, I'll guide you through the broader strategies so that you can begin to identify where you need to focus more attention in your customer experience. Some of the advice may seem obvious, but I've included it because you'd be surprised by how much gets forgotten or overlooked when you're in the startup phase, with a million things on your to-do list and constant fires to put out. The biggest issue I see among cannabis retailers is that they don't even realize when they're making mistakes or when their customer experience needs improvement. Essentially, I want to teach you enough so you know what you don't know. Along the way, though, I'll share best practices and some concrete tips you can implement right now to begin improving your customer experience.

One very big disclaimer before we dive in: *you do not need to do all these things at once.* In fact, it is extraordinarily difficult to implement these strategies all at once, *especially* as a startup. These strategies often cost human resources, money, and time—things that are in short supply for startups. Your customer experience is something you refine and improve throughout the lifetime of your business. This is a marathon, not a sprint, so pace yourself. If you try to tackle everything at once, you and your team will quickly become overwhelmed and potentially burn out. Part of the fine balance of leadership is defining which company priorities to address first. So pick just a few initiatives and focus your efforts there, before moving your team to the next task on the company priority list.

Now let's get started!

Chapter 4

LEADERSHIP

In my corporate career, I've crossed paths with a lot of different leaders. Some of them were exceptional. In the middle of the Office Depot and OfficeMax merger, when everyone was stressed out, one of my leaders was able to bring calm. He united our team and eased our worries. Simultaneously, he prioritized the key merger initiatives while balancing the customer experience. He was excellent at defining the goal, problem solving, coaching for success, and driving accountability. I achieved more than I ever thought possible under his leadership.

I've also seen my share of bad leadership. In fact, a poor leader is a big part of why I began to question remaining in the corporate world. While this individual drove results, with his domineering, almost belittling leadership style, I shriveled up around him. I can talk to anyone about anything all day, but with him, I would stutter and lose my confidence. Instead of bringing out the best in me, he brought out self-doubt. While I still managed to be a star performer despite his influence, I eventually decided that I needed to control my own destiny as an entrepreneur. I left my corporate job on a wing and a prayer that I would find something that would give me purpose. I was open to any industry and had the strong desire to find something new and fulfilling. This openness eventually led me to my long-standing business partner and friend David Kotler, who took a chance on me and eventually inspired me to start my cannabis consulting company, Cannabis Business Growth. Early on, I never could have imagined finding a career in cannabis running my own business, let alone becoming a passionate advocate for the plant.

I am sure that you have had your own experiences with both good and bad leaders. Take a minute to really think back on the impact those individuals had on you, the team, and the company. Now ask yourself, what kind of leader do you want to be?

The way I see it, leadership is like creating a national park. You have all this beautiful wilderness and raw potential around you, and as the leader, you set the trajectory, paving a way through. Bad leaders will either bulldoze straight ahead, which may be efficient but destroys the natural beauty of the wilderness, or they'll carve a challenging, strenuous path, not caring who they leave behind. Great leaders, on the other hand, understand that the best path isn't always straight. The leader's job is to establish a clear direction and remove obstacles so that the team can walk the path easily while experiencing all the beauty the wilderness has to offer. That means sometimes your path will need to curve and wind, or you may need to create multiple paths to fit the needs of different people. The end result is gorgeous vistas and views that take the breath away.

Leadership like this is hard work, but the payoff is huge. If you want to increase revenue, attract more customers, or improve literally any aspect of your store, leadership is where you start.

WHY LEADERSHIP FIRST?

No company is built alone. Your success depends on your team, which means your success depends on leadership. Leadership must come first because it drives every other aspect of the customer experience. The leader sets the tone and creates the culture, and they propel all the initiatives and strategies that will be discussed throughout the remainder of the book. From service to merchandising to promotions, it all trickles down from the leader.

In every company, regardless of industry, leaders have incredible influence. Good leaders make a company, and bad leaders break it. Particularly in the cannabis space, though, leadership is crucial. Our industry is still new, and we don't have best practices or history to draw on. That can be a weakness, but also a strength. It means that, as leaders, we get to build our companies and this industry from the ground up, exactly how we want. It's an exciting position to be in.

The cannabis industry does bring some unique challenges to leadership. First, since accidental success is so common in our space, it's all too easy to overlook the need for a concerted leadership effort. Not realizing the importance of leadership is the number one mistake I see cannabis retailers make. If you're one of the first stores to open in a new market, you could have the neighbor's dog leading the company and still manage to be profitable. Our product sells itself. Eventually, though, as competition increases, you will require strong leadership to remain relevant in the marketplace. Leadership takes time to build, so it's important to start developing these skills now.

Second, while every entrepreneur must deal with uncertainty, it's especially apparent in our industry. Laws, product development, software solutions, banking—everything is constantly changing, and rapidly. With so much uncertainty, a lot of cannabis leaders, particularly those new to leadership roles, have a tendency to cling to control wherever they can. If you're a leader in the cannabis industry, I already know you're a rock star because you have to be able to overcome the permitting and licensing obstacles. But there's a chance you've grown too used to relying on your own skills and abilities to succeed. One of the biggest mistakes I see cannabis leaders make is not delegating. While you might be able to do it all for a short time, eventually you *will* get overwhelmed. Part of becoming a leader is learning how to develop and lean on those around you.

Your leadership will determine how far your company goes. For some people, leadership skills come naturally. Others have to train themselves in at least some of the skills required to lead well. But for all leaders, leadership must be *intentional*.

Let's look at some key leadership strategies and tactics.

THE FIVE FACTORS OF
A WINNING LEADERSHIP MINDSET

If you google "leadership," you'll find hundreds of different definitions and frameworks. Ultimately, every leader is unique, and becoming a great leader means figuring out the particular leadership style that works for you and your store. That said, throughout my career, particularly in the cannabis space, I've found that the most successful leaders share a similar mindset, built on five factors.

#1: Personal Connection

Leadership is ultimately all about people. A leader is nothing without followers, and if you want people to follow you, you have to treat them like—get this—people. No one is going to give you their all if they don't feel some kind of connection with you. Try to approach everyone with fundamental kindness, and work to build real relationships with your team. When you prioritize human connection, you build trust and respect. If you show your team you care about them, they'll care about you too. Plus, the more you understand who someone is—their beliefs, values, and goals—the better you'll know how to motivate them.

#2: Curiosity

A big part of a leader's job is making decisions, which means your brand and store are largely limited by your own imagination. You don't want to reinvent the wheel with every choice you make, but you do want to remain curious and open to new ideas and possibilities. For this reason, the best leaders are always asking questions: Why has a certain team member's performance dropped? What could we be doing differently? Why aren't we doing x? What if we stopped doing y?

#3: Empowerment

Whether you're the CEO or the store manager, as a leader, you are in a position of power. How you use that power determines whether you'll be a good leader or a bad one. Bad leaders hold on to their power; good leaders give it away, empowering their team. Remember that nothing great is accomplished alone. As the leader, it's your job to bring your team members along with you. Your success is measured not by your individual accomplishments, but by your team's.

Micromanagement sucks, and we all know it. It sucks for the people being micromanaged, and it sucks to be the leader doing the micromanaging. There are only so many hours in the day and only so many tasks you can personally accomplish. The more you empower your team, the more time you'll free up to focus on those tasks only you can do. Plus, the more ownership your team members feel for their work, the more invested they'll be. So the best leaders break down the barriers and provide the tools and information their team needs, and then they get out of the way and let their employees do their jobs.

#4: Development

Earlier, I asked you to think about some of the good leaders you've had. I'm going to take a not-so-wild guess here and say that the best leaders you've had, the ones you appreciate the most, helped you grow in some way. What separates average leaders from truly great leaders is that they don't just see their team member's current abilities, but their *potential*. We're all works in progress. If you want your company to keep growing, you want your people to keep growing too. So as a leader, make the development of your people a priority.

#5: Inspiration

There are two levels to how you must inspire your team. First, you must make each individual believe in themselves, which is done through empowerment and development. Second, you must make them believe in the importance of their work, by giving them the *why* behind it. Some whys are fairly tangible: increased sales revenue, improved customer loyalty, better store reviews. Other whys are more intangible: improving the collective health of your customer base, providing education and spreading awareness of mental health issues, giving back to the community. Both whys serve a role. The tangible whys give you goals to work toward, while the intangible whys reveal the deeper mission behind the company, the purpose that makes the work feel meaningful.

Keep these five big-picture strategies front and center, and you're already well on the way to becoming a better leader. We'll spend the remainder of the chapter getting deeper into the *how* of these strategies.

MANAGE YOUR TALENT— IDENTIFY IT, DEVELOP IT, AND RETAIN IT

As a leader, you're in the business of talent—identifying it, hiring it, developing it, and retaining it. Your top priority should thus be your people.

The first place to look to see if you have a people problem in your company is employee turnover. You can't (and shouldn't want to) completely avoid turnover, as it's natural for some employees to move on and, occasionally, you will make hiring mistakes and need to let people go. However, if you have high employee turnover—say, as high as 20 to 30 percent over the course of a year—it's a sign you have an illness in your company. While this figure may seem low, traditional retailers aim for an even lower turnover rate. To calculate turnover, divide the number of employees that left the company by the total number of employees. For instance, if thirty employees out of one hundred employees leave in the course of a year, your turnover is 30 percent.

If your employees don't want to work at your store, do you think they're going to create the kind of environment that customers want to shop in? Probably not. And if a good portion of your employees are in training and don't yet know what they're doing, is that going to create a delightful customer experience? Again, probably not. An employee who has been with your company for two years inherently knows more than someone who has been there for two months, and you can't put a dollar value on that kind of experience, especially in the cannabis space, where sales associates need to be incredibly knowledgeable about the product.

Bottom line, turnover is *expensive*, both financially and culturally. Every time an employee leaves, you have to pay the costs of onboarding and training a new employee. According to Gallup, that cost can range from one-half to two times the employee's annual salary.[70] It's far cheaper—and results in a better customer experience—to retain and develop your current employees. Turnover also damages your company culture. When you have many empty positions or many new employees in training, it increases the pressure and stress on your veteran employees. It can trigger a wildfire of employees leaving, which lowers morale and disrupts team dynamics.

Many factors can contribute to turnover. If you're not offering compensation and perks that are on par with other cannabis retailers in your area, for instance, you're likely to lose employees. The biggest factor, though, is leadership. You might have heard the saying before that people don't leave companies, they leave managers. If your management team makes employees miserable or doesn't make them feel valued, they'll leave. If, on the other hand, you adopt the leadership mindset and take the time to train managers to form a personal connection, be curious, empower, develop, and inspire your employees, they're more likely to stay because those elements create a rewarding, enjoyable work environment.

It's also critical that you establish a practice of promoting from within. If your employees don't see any growth opportunities within your company,

---

[70] Shane McFeely and Ben Wigert, "This Fixable Problem Costs US Businesses $1 Trillion," Gallup, March 13, 2019, https://www.gallup.com/workplace/247391/fixable-problem-costs-businesses-trillion.aspx.

they will be forced to leave to progress in their career. Promoting from within also just makes good business sense. Who knows your store and your company culture better than the people who already work there? When you promote an employee to a leadership position, they can hit the ground running. Especially as you scale, promoting from within is key to implementing a seamless customer experience across multiple locations. At Office Depot, we had an internal promotion plan for how to fill every critical role (which included every leadership role) if the position opened up. When a role is empty, it disrupts the continuity of operations. Imagine a ship whose captain is swept overboard. You need a second-in-command ready to step up and fill the role.

As you hire and build paths to leadership positions for your employees, keep diversity, inclusion, and equity in mind. With the long history of people of color being disproportionately impacted by the War on Drugs, the very least we can do as retailers is ensure we are being fair and creating opportunity in our hiring and promoting practices. Plus, diversity leads to better business results! McKinsey & Company found that companies in the top quartile for ethnic and cultural diversity in executive teams outperformed those in the bottom quartile by *36 percent*.[71]

As unpleasant as it can be, the final aspect of managing the talent of your company is understanding when to let people go. Every employee is a representation of your company and contributes to the customer experience. You can't afford to have subpar employees when you could put someone incredible in that role—someone who will make a difference in terms of how customers think and feel about you.

[71] Sundiatu Dixon-Fyle et al., *Diversity Wins: How Inclusion Matters*, McKinsey & Company, May 19, 2020, https://www.mckinsey.com/featured-insights/diversity-and-inclusion/diversity-wins-how -inclusion-matters.

If a team member isn't living up to the expectations of a role, you need to provide clear, regular feedback about what needs to change. Employ your curiosity and ask leading questions to try to mold them into the role: Why do you do things that way? Have you thought about other ways to do it? What if you tried x or y? If after several months, they're still failing to meet expectations, they're probably not a good fit for the role. At that point, you can either try to find a different role for them if you think they could still make a valuable contribution, or it's time to let them go. You can't expect people to magically know everything they need to know and perform well in a role without guidance and training, but you also can't expect everyone to be a good fit.

As a leader, it's easy to get caught up in the minutiae—emails to answer, decisions to make, spreadsheets to review. Those tasks are important, but the area where you can have the most impact is in people development. When you put people first, it's like dropping a rock into a still pond, spreading ripples throughout the company.

COACH YOUR TEAM

The foundation of people development is coaching. When you coach an employee, you reinforce and encourage their good behaviors while helping them improve their not-so-good behaviors. Coaching is all about development and empowerment, while also giving you opportunities to build personal connections. Here are some tips to help you become a more effective coach.

Coach in the moment as much as possible by incorporating mini coaching sessions throughout the day. The sooner you provide feedback in response to an action, the better, because the coachee will understand exactly what went wrong (or right) and be able to adjust (or cement) the behavior immediately. If you instead save your feedback for a monthly coaching session, you'll overwhelm your coachee with information, and they'll have a harder time translating your coaching advice to the reality of their work.

So when you see someone doing something good, call it out immediately. And when you see something that could be done better, call that out too. Be sure to give constructive criticism privately, and always start with something positive. Tell the coachee what they're doing well, and then build on that, sharing how they can up their game even more. The focus shouldn't be on past mistakes, but on future improvements.

Teach your employees how to accomplish a task; don't do it for them. You've heard the adage: "Give a man a fish, and you feed him for a day. Teach him to fish, and you feed him for a lifetime." Resist the urge to step in and take over your employees' tasks, even if it would be faster or easier than teaching them how to do it themselves. For example, say an employee keeps facing the same problem again and again, and you know you could solve it with a quick phone call to so-and-so. Sure, you could pick up the phone and do it yourself, but it will be far more empowering for you to instead say, "Hey, you know who could probably help with that?" and let the employee make the call themselves to work out the issue.

Show, don't tell. "Show, don't tell" is a key principle in fiction writing, and the same idea applies to coaching. For simple, straightforward feedback —like, "This product goes here, not there"—you can simply tell your employees what needs to be done, but showing, through stories, is a valuable technique for larger or more complex coaching. By sharing a story with the coachee, you can show them *why* a certain action is so important, and if it's a personal story, you'll also build that human connection.

As an example, I was working with an entrepreneur who would snap at his team when he got frustrated. I could've simply said, "Don't do that," but instead, I told him a story about a leader I had. One day, this leader got some *really* bad news in front of our team—but looking at him, you wouldn't even know it. He was the picture of perfect calm, and because of that, the rest of us stayed calm too. Instead of spiraling into anxiety and stress, we got to work fixing the problem. "You're really growing into your leadership position," I explained, "which means people are always looking to you for guidance. How you feel affects how they feel, so your ability to control your emotions is your ability to control your team's emotions." By using this story, I was able to show him why emotional control was so important and give him a clear picture of what kind of leader he had the potential to be if he worked on this one issue.

Encourage team members to become coaches themselves. The ultimate goal as a leader is to make yourself obsolete. The more you develop and empower your team, the less they need you, including as a coach. When a team member excels in a certain area, have them teach that skill to others. You accomplish three important things doing this: (1) you acknowledge their skill, which will give them confidence and make them feel appreciated, (2) you empower them to become a leader themselves (which can help prepare them for a future promotion), and (3) you provide the rest of your staff with more effective coaching because often, your team members are better at that particular skill than you are. For instance, say you have a sales associate struggling to offer personalized recommendations to customers. You might be able to coach them through that, but you know who'd be even better at it? Your top sales associate who gives those kinds of recommendations day in and day out.

No matter your team's current skill level, they can get even better.

Coaching them to the next level is the best, most effective way to improve your customer experience and bottom-line results.

Four Quick-and-Dirty Leadership Tips

1. **Hold a daily standup meeting.** Every day, the store manager should hold a quick ten- to-fifteen-minute meeting with staff. On busy days, especially if the store is running promotions, the meeting functions like a game-day pep talk, getting everyone on the same page. The manager can go over all the discounts that are running and any relevant updates, like restocking plans or products that are currently being highlighted. On nonbusy days, the meetings can include short training sessions, like a refresher on terpenes or a customer role-playing exercise. If you have different shifts of workers, plan to hold multiple standup meetings throughout the day.

2. **Lead by example.** On a regular basis, carve out some time to be visible to your staff so that you can model the kinds of behaviors you want them to display. The easiest way to do this is "walking the store," which is exactly what it sounds like. You walk around the retail space, picking up trash, fixing product displays, interacting with customers, and generally looking for things that could be improved.

3. **Learn people's names and some personal details about them.** This may seem obvious, but it makes such a huge difference. If you're the CEO and you walk into one of your stores and know all the employees' names, it tells them they matter to you. Or say you're a store manager and an employee mentions their grandmother is in the hospital. If you follow up with them later to check in, you're showing them that you care. People nowadays are used to being treated like cogs in a machine; it's up to you

to show them they're more than that. Take the time to speak with every individual you're responsible for leading, and connect with them. If you lead a lot of people, feel free to take notes to jog your memory.

4. **Express gratitude.** People like to be appreciated, so make "thank you" a key part of your vocabulary. For gratitude to be effective, it must be genuine. Don't give out fake or insincere compliments. Instead, pay attention to the good work your employees are doing, and acknowledge it when you see it. Encourage your staff to express gratitude to each other as well.

    Simply saying "thank you" goes a long way, but you can get creative here as well. For instance, one company I worked for used a pin system, in which each level of leader had a different colored set of pins that they could give out to staff in recognition. Have fun with it, and practice being grateful. If you make people feel good about what they're doing, they will continue to grow and do good things for you.

SET GOALS

I'm going to let you in on a secret: people *want* to be led, and they want goals. Doing the same thing, day in and day out, without working toward something bigger is a recipe for burnout and employee disengagement. We're designed to grow, not to be stagnant. So you should be setting goals for your employees—objectives they can work toward and feel proud of accomplishing.

The first step in setting goals is clearly communicating the company's mission. That's the big goal everyone needs to be aligned with and working toward. However, you will also need to set smaller goals to reach that big goal, or you'll easily get overwhelmed. During the Civil War, for example, the big goal for the North was to win the war. To do that, Abraham Lincoln established short-term strategic objectives, like blockading key Southern ports and gaining control of the Mississippi River. His focus was on one battle at a time versus trying to tackle everything at once. You should do the same. Focus on one task or initiative at a time and then move on to the next, slowly racking up small wins.

The goals you set will largely be about company outcomes and results, but they should also be about leadership development. You can't lead by yourself. You need leaders throughout the company, and since leadership skills take time to develop, it's best to start early. Put people in a position to lead before they're in an official leadership position. Give them stretch assignments that come with more responsibility and decision-making authority, like setting up a new point-of-sale-system, creating a training for new products, or reorganizing product placement in the store. This book is filled with suggestions for improving your store, and you're not going to be able to do them all on your own, so it's a perfect opportunity to delegate some stretch assignments.

Work to find that happy middle ground of challenging your team members without overwhelming them. Relinquish control and let them have ownership of the task, but enable their success by being available for coaching and advice. Expect some mistakes because they're bound to happen when we're being stretched and growing. Then, when the employee completes the stretch assignment, remember to celebrate. They've just worked incredibly hard and accomplished something they've never done before, and that deserves recognition!

To be most effective in setting goals, establish regular one-on-one meetings (ideally weekly or biweekly) with your employees where you can talk about their work and where they want to go in their career. If you can align someone's work goals with their personal goals, they will be far more invested.

For example, you might have an assistant manager who has no desire to ever become manager but is interested in pursuing a career in merchandising. Instead of giving that individual stretch assignments related to leadership, it makes much more sense to give them merchandising stretch assignments.

Goals are the key to inspiration. Without goals, your employees will be aimless, treading water. With goals, they'll have a destination to work toward, and they'll be far more likely to succeed.

ESTABLISH OPEN COMMUNICATION

A lot of leadership will be about your one-on-one interactions with your staff, but it's not enough for you to have a good relationship with each of your employees; they also need to have good relationships with each other. Simply put, you need to build a *team*, and you do that through communication.

One of the biggest mistakes I saw again and again in my corporate career was a failure to communicate. I'd frequently encounter situations that could be solved quickly and easily if only people talked to each other. It's so obvious in theory, but in practice, it can be tricky. If people don't have a forum for communication or established relationships with each other (especially if they're in different departments), then their default will be to say nothing. As the leader, then, your job is to open the pathways for communication.

Start by creating a space for people to regularly interact and talk to one another, both within and across teams. It's all too easy for silos to form in the workplace, where each team does its own thing, insulated from the others. To get the best results, though, you need everyone to be communicating. As the CEO, that might mean holding a weekly meeting for all the department heads to discuss big-picture strategy and initiatives, or if you're the store manager, it might be a meeting with both the front-of-house sales associates and the back-of-house inventory folks. Depending on your company, you might also have a digital communication space, like Slack, where employees can ask questions or make suggestions.

Next, on a case-by-case basis as different situations arise, make necessary introductions and put people in contact with each other. Maybe one of your inventory management folks is facing an issue, and to solve it, they really need to talk it out with a vendor. If they've never spoken with that vendor before, they might be nervous or uncertain about reaching out. You can very quickly make the introduction to get the ball rolling. Or maybe you have two different store managers who have been butting heads recently. You can set up a meeting to get them in the same room so they can talk it out.

As you create open lines of communication, remember to stay curious. Communication requires both speaking and listening. Ask questions and don't assume you know everything, because no one does. One thing that will help keep you curious is to get rid of the me-vs-you (or us-vs-them) mentality and coach your team to get rid of it as well. Instead, adopt a mindset of us-vs-the problem.

The people in your company all bring different skills to the table, but only with open communication can you make the most of those strengths. So make sure people are talking to each other.

MAKE AN IMPACT

Great leaders make an impact and bring out the best in their people. Poor leaders are never able to get top performance from their employees, and they often lose their best people to other companies with better leaders.

Running a store is like coaching a sports team. You can run drills, give feedback, and call the plays, but ultimately, you're not the one on the field playing the game. Your team is. They're the ones out there achieving results, and your job is to give them the tools for success. You have to develop, empower, and inspire them so they can go out there, give it their all, and win the game, which in this case means creating an incredible customer experience.

As a leader, you can make a larger impact than you ever could alone—on your store, on your team members, and on the customer experience. When it's done right, leadership lifts everyone up, yourself included.

Chapter 5

BRANDING

I used to be a Qdoba customer. I was in love with their tortilla soup (which has since been discontinued) and had it for lunch all the time. Then a Chipotle opened in my area. I ordered Chipotle every once in a while, but I was still a Qdoba girl. After all, Chipotle didn't have tortilla soup, so it would be a hard battle to win me over as a customer. Over time, though, that's exactly what happened: my loyalty shifted from Qdoba to Chipotle. Why? Chipotle's branding.

When I first started eating at Chipotle, their hook for me was the food. Simply put, it tasted good. Then I learned their ingredients were organically and ethically sourced, with no hormones or artificial junk added. As a busy mom, I don't always have time to cook meals, which means I have to make a choice about what kind of fast food to feed my daughter. Some guilt can come along with that, but with Chipotle, I don't have to feel guilty. I'm feeding her food that is natural and healthy. She's getting her vegetables, her protein, and all the nutrients she needs, and she likes it, because it's delicious!

All these things I love about Chipotle ultimately came back to the brand. Chipotle's brand is all about being real: real ingredients, real purpose, real flavor. They've woven that concept into every aspect of the company. You can see it on their bags and cups, in the way they source ingredients, in their commitment to reducing landfill waste, and in how they treat their employees. If you have a Chipotle account, you can even go online and see your "foodprint," in which they show you how much carbon you've offset and water you've saved by choosing Chipotle. As a busy, health-focused, and environmentally conscious mom, Chipotle's brand speaks to me in everything they do. They make me *feel good*, as a person and as a mom, about spending my money there.

Since your brand impacts how the customer feels about you—and themselves—it's an absolutely critical aspect of the customer experience.

YOUR BRAND = YOUR NORTH STAR

Your brand is your north star. It is who you are as a company. Perhaps an even better way to look at it is that your brand is *who you want to be*. As such, your brand should guide every decision you make. The way your employees interact with customers, how your store looks, the products you stock, how you design your website, the way you run promotions—it's all connected to your brand.

Branding is hugely important because it lets us influence how we're perceived, not just individually but as an industry. So branding serves two purposes: (1) to help us hook customers and encourage their loyalty, and (2) to change the stigma around cannabis. I believe that, as retailers, it's our responsibility to prioritize both of these goals. That's why I was so disappointed in the cannabis company I spoke about in Chapter 3 that went the "sex sells" route, with the scantily clad women. I already pointed out how that kind of branding can hurt us as an industry, but it's also worth mentioning that it can hurt our *customers* too. Your brand is your public image. It is something both customers and noncustomers can be aware of. Imagine if giant cannabis billboards with scantily clad women were put up in your community. What impression of cannabis would that convey, particularly to people who are already prejudiced against cannabis users? Would those billboards show them the truth about cannabis and cannabis users or reinforce all the stereotypes our customers have to deal with?

When a customer spends their hard-earned dollars in your store, they are essentially endorsing you. They are choosing to associate themselves with you, perhaps not publicly, but at least in their own mind. So your brand is not just your own identity as a company. It's also a reflection of at least some small part of your customers' identity. That's a big deal! *Especially* in cannabis. With so much shame floating around, if you can create a brand that customers are proud to associate with, it's *huge* and will go a long way in developing customer loyalty and breaking the stigma.

Your brand will influence every aspect of the customer experience, so it's important to spend the time to clearly and carefully define what your brand represents. Every company's brand will be a little different, but the most successful brands I've seen all share four pillars in their branding.

PILLAR #1: BE INCLUSIVE

Recently, there's been a push in branding to become more targeted, zeroing in on a specific niche of customers. The idea is that if you try to appeal to everyone, you end up with a weak, bland message that appeals to no one.

This is good advice for many companies, but for cannabis retailers, I caution you against that strategy. Inclusivity is typically a better choice for us because we don't have a single type of customer.

If you try to zero in on a niche, you're going to end up alienating a sizable chunk of your customer base. Many of our potential customers already struggle with the fact that they don't fit into the mold of the stereotypical cannabis user. Branding that appeals only to the stereotypical user will not attract them and can even repel them. First-time or novice users in particular may be afraid or nervous to visit a dispensary. If your branding isn't inclusive, they won't feel welcome and may never even step foot in your store, and now you've lost a potential lifetime customer.

As retailers, we really cannot afford to alienate customers. With the rise of the behemoth Amazon, brick-and-mortar stores have continued to see a decline in retail foot traffic. Macy's and Nordstrom have both closed stores, and Brooks Brothers, J.Crew, GNC, JCPenney, Neiman Marcus, Guitar Center, and Pier 1 are among a laundry list of retailers who filed bankruptcy in 2020; generally speaking, traditional brick-and-mortar retail is dying. Currently, cannabis is an exception to this trend, in large part because of legal restrictions on how cannabis can be sold. Even so, if you create a brand designed to target a narrow segment of the population, like twenty-five- to thirty-year-old men, you are limiting yourself.

All this said, if you really want to go niche, you *can* do it. There are successful cannabis retailers out there who have chosen that path. Just understand that if you're going to go niche, you need to do it really well because you're starting with a much smaller potential customer base. One alternative you might consider is to go with an inclusive overall brand and then create micro-experiences within your store that appeal to specific customer groups. While retailers are better off being inclusive, the niche strategy can be very effective for cannabis products. The Heavy Hitters brand is a good example. They have a clear target customer—people, primarily men, who want the strongest, toughest products. By stocking a variety of targeted products like this, you can appeal to multiple niche groups.

Even with a goal of being inclusive, you shouldn't expect to appeal to *everyone*. Chipotle's brand of being real is inclusive because it can speak to people regardless of race, gender, age, and so on, but that doesn't mean everyone is going to be a Chipotle fan. The point of inclusivity is to ensure that your branding is not purposely or accidentally excluding entire segments of your customer base. By choosing an inclusive branding message, you can make your store a welcoming place for your many varied customers.

PILLAR #2:
HAVE A PURPOSE GREATER THAN PROFIT

Look, we all want to make money, and in the cannabis industry, we have the opportunity to make a lot of it. In my work with cannabis companies, increasing profit is absolutely a priority. But—and this is a big but—profit *cannot* be your only purpose. Every business wants to make money. If you want to stand out and compete in this space, you need something more to make you unique. We've also seen what happens when companies prioritize profit and profit alone. In my opinion, this profit tunnel vision was a key contributor to pharmaceutical companies pushing the addictive drugs that created the Opioid Endemic. We have to be better than that. We have to earn respect from both customers and the public as a whole, and one way to do that is using our brands to actively do good in our communities and the world.

A brand used to just be the experience a customer had with the company, but it's bigger now, in part due to the rise of conscious capitalism, an idea presented by Whole Foods co-founder John Mackey and marketing professor Raj Sisodia. Conscious capitalism is the idea that companies should operate ethically, serving not just their shareholders but all their employees and the larger world as a whole. Customers today have access to more information about companies than ever before, and they're putting their wallets where their values are. Companies have lost revenue due to social issues and value clashes with customers. As an example, I personally stopped eating at Jimmy John's when I found out that the founder and owner, Jimmy John Liautaud, hunted endangered species in Africa. Even though I think their sandwiches are delicious, I couldn't have my money supporting that.

Conscious capitalism is especially important for us cannabis retailers because of the stigma we're dealing with. It's not enough for us to disprove the Big Lie that cannabis is dangerous. We have to show people that cannabis is not only safe but *beneficial* for users and society as a whole. While I do think we have a responsibility to use our platforms as retailers and business owners to better the world, purpose shouldn't feel like a burden or something you *have* to do. It's something you should *want* to do, for your personal fulfillment. Take Betty Mitchell, the CEO of Tively who was gracious enough to share her story and insights with me for this book (see the sidebars in Chapters 1 and 2). A big reason she decided to go all-in on her cannabis venture while in her sixties was so she could further her nonprofit work and help foster children. Your purpose can be anything you want it to be. Maybe you want to support the local arts, further human rights, assist the elderly, or contribute to the Black Lives Matter movement. Your purpose also doesn't have to be some huge social issue. Perhaps you want to help people have fun in a stress-filled world, celebrate hip-hop music, or sell the highest-quality products available—those are still purposes bigger than profit alone.

If you're struggling to find a purpose, think about how you want customers to feel when they come into your store. You want them to give their money to you, not any other cannabis store. What are you going to give them in return that other stores don't? The answer to that can likely develop into your purpose. Your purpose may also change over time. As long as you show customers that you care about more than just profit, you're headed in the right direction.

What Cannabis Can Do for Veterans: Purpose in Action

An example of what it looks like for a cannabis retailer to have a purpose greater than profits is Cake's commitment to serving veterans.

On average, about eighteen veterans commit suicide each day, which translates to a suicide rate 1.5 times higher than the average population.[72] Military service is *difficult*. Many service members are young, just eighteen years old, when they first enlist. They're thrown into a brutal, cutthroat environment where they're surrounded by violence. To survive, they have to become emotionally dead. This is necessary to an extent because they are training for war, but it also breeds mental illness.

Upon returning home, many veterans face PTSD, anxiety, and depression, in addition to potential physical injuries that require pain management. Simultaneously, much of the camaraderie and support they felt during their

---

[72] US Department of Veterans Affairs, Office of Mental Health and Suicide Prevention, *2020 National Veteran Suicide Prevention Annual Report*, November 2020, retrieved May 21, 2021, https://www.mentalhealth.va.gov/mentalhealth/suicide_prevention/data.asp.

service disappears. It can feel like they're all on their own as they try to rebuild their lives. So it is no wonder why they suffer from a higher suicide rate, as well as higher rates of alcoholism and opioid overdoses.[73]

Cannabis has proved effective in treating many of the physical and mental issues veterans face. For instance, one recent scientific study funded by the Colorado Department of Public Health and Environment and involving researchers from multiple prestigious universities, including Johns Hopkins School of Medicine, followed a group of individuals with PTSD over one year to look at the effects of cannabis use. The participants who used cannabis not only reported a greater decrease in the severity of their PTSD symptoms but were also 2.57 times more likely to recover from their PTSD over the course of the study compared to the nonusers.[74]

Unfortunately, due to cannabis's Schedule I status, many veterans and current service members do not have access to it. Current service members not only lack access but face severe punishment for cannabis use, including discharge and the loss of all their benefits. While cannabis use is becoming more socially accepted among veterans, the VA (Veterans Affairs), as a federally funded entity, does not offer cannabis as an option, and many veterans fear they could still be punished for using cannabis, just as they would be if on active duty.

As a naval veteran, Daniel Wise, Cake's CEO and co-founder, understands the challenges veterans face and has made serving this at-risk community a key part of Cake's mission. Cake offers daily discounts to veterans and

---

[73] "Substance Use and Military Life," National Institute on Drug Abuse, October 2019, https://www.drugabuse.gov/publications/drugfacts/substance-use-military-life.

[74] Marcel O. Bonn-Miller et al., "The Long-Term, Prospective, Therapeutic Impact of Cannabis on Post-Traumatic Stress Disorder," *Cannabis and Cannabinoid Research* (2020), https://doi.org/10.1089/can.2020.0056.

supports California's SB-34, the Dennis Peron and Brownie Mary Act, which allows Cake to provide cannabis products to veterans free of charge. This is because Wise believes that providing veterans access to cannabis will set off a domino effect of positive benefits. With less mental and physical pain, they will be better able to function in daily life. They'll be less likely to turn to alcohol and other drugs to numb their pain, and they'll have better chances of securing employment and taking the steps to live fulfilling, successful lives, ultimately translating to fewer veteran suicides. That is purpose in action.

PILLAR #3: BE AUTHENTIC

Inclusivity and purpose will be at the center of your brand. From there, you can build out your brand strategy in many directions. You could be funny or weird. You could focus on education and the science behind cannabis. You could prioritize an all-natural, organic image. You could go for warm and fuzzy feelings. Your overall strategy and tone of branding should align with your purpose—if your purpose is, say, supporting local artists, it wouldn't make sense or feel authentic to have a store designed like a clean, minimalist laboratory. So your purpose will guide your strategy, but you still have a lot of freedom and space to be creative.

Just look at Death Wish Coffee. Their brand is built on having the strongest coffee—so strong you must have a death wish to drink it. I'm not a coffee drinker myself, but I still subscribe to Death Wish Coffee's marketing emails, because they're so hilarious. They've chosen to go fun and over-the-top with their branding. In 2018, they even sent some of their coffee to the International Space Station so they could lay claim to having the world's strongest coffee in the galaxy. Come on, that's amazing! I'm not the only one completely hooked by their branding. I first learned about Death Wish from one of my clients. He loves their coffee so much he wants to open a Death Wish–branded coffee shop, just so he can swing by for a fresh, hot cup on his way to work. That's some impressive customer loyalty right there!

Death Wish's branding works because it's authentic to the company. They easily could have gone in a different direction. They could have chosen to be more serious, focusing on the research that went into creating their coffee or branding it as a luxury product. If you listen to CEO and founder Mike Brown speak, though, that kind of branding wouldn't feel as authentic to the company. Brown is down-to-earth and doesn't take himself too seriously. He has a great sense of humor, and overall, the staff and company have a cool, rebel vibe. You can feel how the branding is a true reflection of the company and its people.

Humans are social creatures. We can bond with just about anything—animals, Roombas, and yes, companies too. In order for people to bond with you, though, you need to be authentic. If you're a funny person, lean into that for your branding, or if you wear your heart on your sleeve in everything you do, then make sure that's reflected in your branding. The more authentic you are to yourself, the more unique your branding will end up being, which will help you stand out and connect with customers.

PILLAR #4:
USE STORY TO BUILD TRUST AND CONNECTION

People are naturally drawn to stories. They evoke emotion and stick in our heads. The story of your company is one of your best opportunities to form a connection with your customers and build trust, in addition to communicating your higher purpose beyond profits.

A perfect example of the power of story is Charlotte's Web CBD. The company was founded by the seven Stanley brothers, and in their words, "We didn't start as a company. We started as a mission."[75] The company's name of course brings to mind the beloved children's book *Charlotte's Web*, but it was also named after a little girl, Charlotte Figi. Charlotte suffered from a drug-resistant form of epilepsy and could have up to hundreds of seizures a week. The Stanley brothers owned a medical marijuana dispensary in Colorado and had worked to cultivate an optimal high-CBD, low-THC strain for medicinal purposes. Charlotte's mother reached out to them in the hope they could help her daughter. They developed a CBD tincture for Charlotte, and it worked. Her seizures dropped drastically, to just a few per month.

Charlotte's story received global media attention and helped to spark a shift in public perception and laws related to CBD. Thousands began flocking to Colorado in order to have access to the Stanley brothers' CBD tincture. The brothers gave away the tincture to those it could help, and eventually, demand rose so high that they founded Charlotte's Web. Today the company is a registered B Corp, meaning it's a business that balances profit and purpose, meeting the highest standards of social and environmental performance. The brothers' higher purpose is "to unleash the healing powers of botanicals with compassion and science, benefiting the planet and all who live upon it."[76] You can see that purpose in their story and in their various social and environmental initiatives, from employing organic and regenerative farming practices to partnering with nonprofits.

---

[75] "About Us," Charlotte's Web, accessed June 21, 2021, https://www.charlottesweb.com/about-us.

[76] "About Us," Charlotte's Web.

The Stanley brothers' story reveals the soul of the company. When I think of Charlotte's Web, I don't think of a cold, impersonal business; I think of the very real people who make up the company. Because of that, I *trust* Charlotte's Web. I know they are committed to helping people and producing a quality CBD product. Particularly in our industry, because of the stigma that has created fear and worry around cannabis, trust is essential. I could go online and find lots of CBD options, but who knows if they'll be legitimate. The unfortunate reality is that many CBD products today are no more than snake oil, which is damaging to our industry as a whole. With Charlotte's Web, you know exactly what you're getting and what you're supporting, and that makes it easy to spend your money there.

As a sad coda to this story, Charlotte passed away in 2020, due to what were likely complications related to COVID-19.

Three Quick-and-Dirty Branding Tips from Betty Mitchell

Betty Mitchell, CEO of Tively, is a branding master, and she shared three of her best branding tips for new retailers:

1. **On Names.** Your name shouldn't be more than three syllables. Start by reading as much as you can about what you do. There is a word somewhere in there that describes what you do without describing what you do. For instance, my business name is Tively—*positively*, without the first four letters.
2. **On Logos and Taglines.** Look at other logos out there through Google Images. Find three or four you like, and use that as the inspiration for your

own design. Create your own amalgamation, combining color schemes, fonts, imagery, and so on. And look at brand taglines, then create your own by mixing up the words. Try to stay under seven syllables.

3. **On Packaging**. Go for dignity in your packaging. I see so many eighth bags, and I find them so silly and childish. Packaging makes a big impression on the customer, so choose products that look professional.

WEAVE YOUR BRANDING INTO EVERYTHING

Once you've established your four pillars, you will have the start of a strong brand. The next step is to weave it into every aspect of your company. Going back to Death Wish Coffee, you can see their brand in their name (Death Wish Coffee), logo (skull and crossbones), story (about the founder Mike Brown seeing a need at his small coffee shop for stronger, but still delicious, coffee to wake up his groggy morning customers), marketing (funny emails), and more. If your branding isn't consistent across the company, it won't feel as authentic or be as effective.

There are lots of ways to weave your branding into your company, but one of the first you should consider is your name. A name can seem like a small thing, but names are important. Your name is the customer's first introduction to your identity, so it should reflect your brand in some way. As an example, I work with a cannabis brand called Cake. A lot of thought went into that name. First, some of the most popular cannabis strains among consumers are "cake" strains: wedding cake, lemon cake, apple cake, and so on. Second, when you think of cake, you think of celebration and happiness. Third, among the younger crowd, *cake* can mean money or a fine booty. The icing on top of this cake? The name for the brand's stores will be The Cake House, or TCH, which naturally brings to mind THC. With just a name, Cake is appealing to multiple demographics and establishing a brand identity centered around celebration and joy.

After your name, consider your logo and tagline. Does your logo make sense with your brand? For instance, if your brand is all about joy, you're not going to want a ton of dark colors in your logo, or if your brand is centered around the arts, you better have a cool, artsy logo. Your tagline is a short phrase that sums up your brand. Keep it to a few words, and make it memorable. Death Wish Coffee's tagline is "The World's Strongest Coffee," and Chipotle's is "Chipotle, for Real."

After figuring out the branding basics (name, logo, and tagline), keep your brand in mind as you make all your decisions as a company. Your staff uniform, the products you stock, the art you put on the walls, the material you put on your website—it should all be informed by your brand. The sooner you establish your brand, the better you'll be able to embed it into your company.

PROTECT YOUR BRAND

As you develop and implement your brand, you need to protect it. Your brand is a key part of your company that you will spend years building, and if it's damaged, repairing it will take a lot of time and work. Better to get out in front of potential issues and prevent the damage in the first place.

Start by making sure you're not infringing on anyone else's trademarks or intellectual property. Check to make sure your name isn't already taken and that your logo isn't too similar to anyone else's, especially if you used other companies' logos for inspiration. You might think it's not a big deal, but if you get slapped with a lawsuit, you're going to change your tune very quickly. These kinds of lawsuits can and do happen in the industry. One of the most famous involved the company Gorilla Glue, which successfully negotiated a settlement in which the involved cannabis company had to stop using the word "gorilla" and associated imagery in its cannabis strains.

On the flip side, you also want to do the legal work to protect your own intellectual property. Get a lawyer to submit your trademarks and doing-business-as (DBAs). Otherwise, you could pour years into building your brand, only to have some other company come in and take your name. All of a sudden, you might no longer be the only or first result when customers try to google you. The other company could even force you to change your name, and you'll have to redo all the name recognition you've built in your community.

Aside from the legal aspects, protecting your brand means protecting your reputation. Actions speak louder than words. If you say you stand for one thing but do another, customers will eat you alive. If you're the CEO, this applies to your personal actions as well. You're the leader, so your actions reflect on the company. I know of a couple of cannabis CEOs who have lawsuits against them for misogyny and sexual harassment. Those lawsuits have made it into the news, which means that information is available to customers, who very well may choose to take their business elsewhere as a result. A damaged reputation is a big deal because rebuilding customer loyalty is a lot harder than simply retaining it. For instance, Jimmy John's founder, Liautaud, has apparently not hunted big game in many years, but I still don't eat at his restaurants. They lost my loyalty and haven't been able to rebuild it.

Your brand is truly priceless. It's one of your most valuable assets as a retailer, so protect it.

BUILD YOUR BRAND OVER TIME

When you first start your company, you need to establish some aspects of your brand right away. No one's going to open their doors without a name, for instance. After figuring out the basics, though, many retailers let their brand fall by the wayside. This is a mistake. Your brand must be cultivated throughout the lifetime of your company. Just as people grow and change, your company will too. Your brand will need to evolve with it.

Use the four pillars of cannabis branding—being inclusive, having a higher purpose, being authentic, and using story to build trust and connection—to get a clear idea of who you are as a company. Once you understand who you are, you'll be better able to communicate your identity to customers and transcend beyond the "give money, get cannabis" interaction to a real customer *experience*.

Chapter 6

SERVICE

The moment someone finds out I work in the cannabis industry, a countdown clock starts. It's only a matter of time before they pull me aside privately. The conversation always starts in vague, uncertain whispers:

"Hey, could we talk?" Then the barrage of questions starts.

"I have anxiety (or depression, pain, or _____)—can cannabis help?"

"What's the difference between indica and sativa?"

"Do different strains matter?"

"How do I ingest it? Smoke it? Vape it? Eat it?"

"Will my neighbors be able to smell it?"

"Can I take too much? What happens if I do?"

"How much will it cost?"

"When I go to a store, what do I *do*? What do I ask for? How much do I ask for?"

"What is a terpene?"

If this kind of thing happened only once or twice, I wouldn't think much of it, but it happens *all the time*. Some of it is due to my personality. I don't know what it is about me, but I'll go to the gas station, and before I walk out, somebody will have told me their whole life story. I will get to chatting with an old lady in line at the grocery store, and by the time I leave, I know all about her children and grandchildren. It happens so regularly that if I'm late returning from an errand, my partner will just laugh and ask, "Who'd you meet this time?"

It's more than that, though. I bet you've gotten very similar questions before. Because of the Big Lies we've been told, misinformation is rampant, and everything to do with cannabis has been hush-hush for so long that people feel uncomfortable talking about it. The result is that many people have lots of questions bottled up inside. They are curious about the truth and they want answers, but they're scared and embarrassed to ask. They are afraid of being judged, both for using cannabis and also, in a strange way, for *not* having used cannabis before. Especially with all the cannabis-specific jargon, they are worried they will be made to feel stupid. They may also feel shame for turning to cannabis to overcome issues they're dealing with, like anxiety.

With the stigma of cannabis and so many emotions at play, we retailers have our work cut out for us. The sheer magnitude of questions I get reveals an unmet need in the cannabis space. Not everyone has a Char in their life that they can pull aside to ask discreet questions, so it's our job as retailers to address this unmet need through our service.

THE NEED FOR TRUSTED, INCLUSIVE, AND EXPERT SERVICE

Service is the cornerstone of any retail experience, but it's particularly important in the cannabis industry for six big reasons:

1. **The stigma.** Because of the stigma, many new users feel intimidated and even scared by cannabis. Any time emotions, especially ones like shame and fear, are involved in a retail experience, the impacts of service are magnified. If a customer comes in already feeling vulnerable and then receives poor service, it will be a *terrible* experience, and they'll probably never come back. At the other end of the spectrum, if your employees can make that person feel safe and comfortable, you could win a customer for life.

2. **The effects of cannabis.** Cannabis is incredibly safe, but it needs to be used properly. When you think about service in cannabis, you have to consider not only the experience inside your store, but the experience outside of it too. For instance, if a new user doesn't understand how long edibles can take to kick in, they could easily take too much and have a very unpleasant experience, which could turn them off of cannabis entirely. Unfortunately, because cannabis is still listed as a Schedule I drug and has not been fully embraced as a medical alternative, our sales associates are sometimes even placed in the tricky position of providing what amounts to medical advice, like which strains are best for those suffering from anxiety. That's a tremendous amount of responsibility.

3. **The broad customer base.** There is no one single type of cannabis user. Your employees must be able to help a wide variety of customers—complete novices and lifelong users, college-aged partiers and grandmothers. Being able to quickly identify different types of customers and adapt to meet their needs requires a high level of service.

4. **The complexity of the product.** If you go to buy milk, you have a few different options to consider. Skim, 2 percent, whole? Organic or not? But mostly, milk is milk. With a product like cannabis, the decision gets more complicated. You have to consider THC levels, CBD levels, terpene profiles, and method of consumption, just to name a few. Even for more experienced users, that's a lot to keep track of! Your employees must become subject matter experts in order to guide customers to the right product.

5. **Product variety.** When you first start out, you might have a limited selection of products, but as the market matures, you will easily have *hundreds*, possibly even thousands, of products in your store. That level of choice allows you to meet the needs of many different kinds of consumers, but it can also be overwhelming from the customer's perspective. In many retail experiences, the customer chooses the product. In cannabis retail, though, because of the sheer quantity of options, the sales associate will often narrow the customer's choices down to just a few targeted recommendations, based on the customer's needs and wants. So essentially, the sales associate is choosing the product for the customer, which makes service extra important.

6. **The newness of the market.** Because the cannabis market is still new, products are changing at a rapid pace. Different strains rise

and fall in popularity, brand-new products are constantly being developed, and current products sometimes become obsolete. With everything in flux, we need to be ready to offer alternatives if a product becomes unavailable and to alert customers to new developments in cannabis.

Because of all the unique aspects and challenges to our product, our service needs to be on an entirely different level from many other retailers. We must build trust with the customer to overcome their fears and worries; create an environment of inclusion so that *all* our customers, from the novice to the connoisseur, feel comfortable and welcome; and be educated enough to provide expert advice. As retailers, we're on the front lines of breaking the stigma against cannabis, and our service employees, whether you call them budtenders or sales associates, are the vanguard. They're the ones directly interfacing with customers, which means they can have a huge impact in breaking the stigma, creating a delightful customer experience, and ultimately building loyalty and increasing sales. So let's look at some strategies to improve service.

GREET THE CUSTOMER

We'll start with a simple but important tip: greet every customer who walks in the door. Your greeting is a customer's first impression of your store. A warm welcome and a smile can go a long way to easing a customer's worries and making them feel more comfortable. In most states, you're required to check customers' IDs as they enter anyway, so it's easy to add a greeting.

The greeting is a perfect opportunity to begin assessing the type of customer you're working with so you can tailor the experience to their needs. A great question to ask is "Have you been in before?" If the answer is yes, then you know they're probably not a first-time user, and you can say, "Welcome back!" If the answer is no, it could be a sign they'll need a bit more guidance, and you might decide to pass them off directly to a sales associate, saying something like, "Welcome in! Karl will help you out and can answer any questions you might have."

Different states have different rules about how products can be displayed in-store. If your store is set up to allow browsing, the greeting is also a chance to: (1) determine whether the customer needs time to browse first and, in the case of new customers, (2) give them a rough guide to how the store is laid out. Don't assume that customers, particularly new ones, will be able to figure things out for themselves. For instance, some stores can't display all their products, either for legal reasons or simple space reasons, so browsing is done via tablets, but if no one tells the customer that's what the tablets are for, they're going to be very confused.

In assessing customers, you should also teach your employees to practice reading body language. New users often seem nervous or uncomfortable, while more experienced users tend to walk and carry themselves like they know what they're looking for. Different customers give off different energies, and a good greeter will learn how to pick up on that.

NAIL THE SALES ASSOCIATE–CUSTOMER INTERACTION

After the greeting, initial assessment, and any browsing that's needed, it's time for the one-on-one sales associate–customer interaction, which should be adapted according to the type of customer: novice, connoisseur, and everyone in between.

The first step of the interaction is thus identifying where the customer is in their cannabis journey. You may already have a rough idea based on the greeting assessment and their body language. From there, ask an open-ended question like "What are you looking for today?" or "What are you interested in?" The answer to that will be your guide for the remainder of the interaction. A novice user might answer, "I'm not sure" or identify themselves as a new user, while a more experienced user will respond with something specific. You can then tailor the interaction according to the customer.

Novice Customers

Walking into a cannabis store can be overwhelming for first-time users. I remember my first time visiting a dispensary. I felt embarrassed and like people were going to judge me for being there. I knew it was ridiculous— after all, everyone there was in a dispensary too, so why would they judge me?—but I still felt uncomfortable. I also felt like I didn't belong. Everyone else seemed to know what they were doing, while I was completely lost. Sativa, indica, flower, buds, sublinguals…*what?*

Because first-time users tend to come in with little knowledge but big emotions, serving them typically takes more time and patience. The goal of the interaction is to make them feel welcome and unjudged and to properly educate them on what they need to know. It's very important that you not rush this interaction. If your store traffic is heavy or you don't have enough staff to accommodate novice users without a long line building up, you need to adjust something. Long lines and waits are not an enjoyable customer experience, and line buildups naturally pressure sales associates to move more quickly through customers. You could schedule additional staff, or you could set up "fast lanes" for customers who have ordered ahead or already know exactly what they want and "slow lanes" for the customers who want to spend more time speaking to a sales associate. You could even consider giving customers the option to schedule consultations, which is particularly common for medical cannabis.

Here are some tips for working with new users:

- **Keep explanations simple, and be careful with cannabis-specific jargon.** You don't want to overwhelm new users with information. They won't be able to remember it all, and it could increase their anxiety. Stick to the basic concepts like sativa, indica, and hybrid. Some people may be too embarrassed to ask about what different words mean, so include brief explanations of the terms you use.

- **Avoid asking questions they won't know the answer to.** A common piece of sales advice is to ask questions and let the customer drive the interaction. You need to be careful with novice users, though, or you'll end up asking lots of questions they can only answer "I don't know" to, which can be frustrating for them. Give them the information they need to answer the question before asking. For instance, instead of asking them what price range they're looking at, first tell them the range of prices you offer for a given product type. That will give them context to help answer the question.

- **Give them just a few recommendations, and help them make the choice if they're struggling.** Novice users will rely on you a lot when it comes to picking their products. Give them only a couple of options, and explain how each option is different in a way they'll understand. If they still seem to be struggling with the choice, tell them which one is your top recommendation. Don't just choose the most expensive. Make it a real recommendation. In deciding what options to present to the customer, there are two big questions you need to help them answer:

> **What kind of experience are they looking for?** Relaxing, uplifting, creative? Something to ease pain or anxiety? New users might not understand the terminology, but they'll probably be able to tell you how they want to feel while using cannabis.

> **What method of consumption will be best for them?** Start with a high-level decision on smoking vs edible vs topical. The choice will be based on the experience they're looking for (e.g., if they don't want to get high, then topical is likely the best choice, or perhaps a CBD edible) and their past experience with various consumption methods (e.g., if they've smoked cigarettes before, smoking will feel natural to them, and pre-rolls in particular could be a good fit). Once you've picked a broad use category, you can get more specific. Maybe they are comfortable smoking but are worried about smell— then vaping might be best. Or maybe they're most comfortable taking an edible, but they want to have a lot of control over portion size—a tincture or beverage, with variable serving sizes, could be a good option, as opposed to a 10 milligram THC candy.

- **Give them clear instructions for how to use the product.** A person's first experiences with cannabis will define their views on it. Set them up for success by walking them through exactly how to use the product. Regardless of consumption method, encourage them to start small (they can always take more), and for edibles specifically, make sure they understand how long they can take to kick in.

- **Ask if they have any concerns.** Keep an eye on their body language throughout the interaction. If they seem to be getting confused or overwhelmed, check in with them. Then end the conversation by asking if they have any concerns or questions that haven't been addressed. As you establish trust with them through the interaction, they'll be more willing to open up about potential fears and worries. Never make them feel stupid for any of their questions, and calmly reassure them as needed.

While working with new users typically takes more time, these interactions can be very rewarding. If you can ease their fears and make them feel welcome, they're usually appreciative, and you very well may turn them into a customer for life.

Connoisseurs

On the opposite end of the spectrum, you have your connoisseurs, people who have been using cannabis for a significant amount of time and are experts in their own right. If you follow the novice script with these experienced users, you're going to create an awful customer experience. Imagine you've been using cannabis for more than a decade and the sales associate spends five minutes explaining the difference between indicas and sativas. That would be pretty annoying, right? Like mansplaining, but with cannabis—cannasplaining?

With connoisseurs, you want to let them drive the conversation. They know what they like and what they're looking for. You don't need to explain terminology or different consumption methods. Your job is simply to match them with the right products and, if possible, introduce them to something new. Here are some tips for working with connoisseurs:

- **Know your stuff.** For connoisseurs, having a high level of knowledge is critical. Be prepared to talk about individual strains, THC percentages, terpene profiles, and so on. If a connoisseur comes away from a retail interaction feeling like they know more than you, they're not going to feel delighted. If a connoisseur asks a question you don't know the answer to, instead of saying, "I don't know," say, "That's a great question—let me find out."
- **Focus on specialty products and new offerings.** Connoisseurs tend to have tried-and-true favorites but also enjoy trying out new things. They often find joy in the newest strains and innovative products.
- **Let them know about deals.** Since connoisseurs often consume a decent amount of cannabis, they tend to appreciate a good deal and often want to buy in bulk. If you can offer them the best product at a competitive price, they're more likely to return to your store.

Connoisseurs can be a lot of fun to work with because you can talk shop with them, and they tend to have a high customer lifetime value (the total amount of money a customer is expected to spend at your business over their lifetime), so it's important to delight them.

In-Betweeners and Other Groups

Your customers may fall on any point of the scale between novice and connoisseur. For these intermediate users, blend the techniques. Ask questions to figure out what they're looking for and get a feel for their current knowledge level. Let them set the pace of the conversation. Some will just want to get in and out, in which case you should provide recommendations quickly. Others will want to chat more, and you can spend some time on education and explanations of different products, tailoring the conversation based on their current knowledge level.

Aside from categorizing people based on their level of experience with cannabis, you might discover other ways to group your customers. For instance, maybe you have a lot of veterans who come into the store. They will have unique needs, and you can look for trends in the types of products they like the most in order to best serve this subset of your customers. Periodically take the time to analyze who your customers are and their trends in purchasing. Talk to your sales associates about what they've noticed so you can pool your collective knowledge to best serve all your customers.

Every customer is unique, but by understanding the patterns and having tips for working with different types of customers, your sales associates can provide a higher level of service.

Provide a Cannabis Usage Journal

One of the big challenges our customers face, particularly in new markets, is figuring out what they like. A cannabis usage journal can help. It provides a structured format for users to record their experiences with different cannabis strains and products. Giving your customers a cannabis usage journal, whether it's an actual physical journal or something digital they print off for themselves, can set you apart from competitors and create a delightful customer experience.

A cannabis usage journal should include questions like this:

- What did I take?
- When did I take it (date and time of day)?

- What was my expected effect?
- What was my actual effect?
- On a scale of 1–10, how would I rate my experience?

To take it to the next level, you might consider pairing the journal with a sampler pack of products, similar to a wine or beer tasting. Not only is this fun for customers, but it gives them a chance to discover products they really love, which ultimately funnels back into more sales for you.

UPSELL AND CROSS-SELL THE RIGHT WAY

A key principle in retail is upselling (suggesting a customer buy a higher-quality, more expensive product) and cross-selling (suggesting a customer buy an additional product). Both of these strategies make you more profitable, but increased profit can't be your only motivation, or you're going to create a poor customer experience. For upselling and cross-selling to be most effective, you need to do them in a way that delights the customer.

As an example, when I was at Office Depot, sales associates were required to ask customers at checkout, "Do you need stamps or paper?" Our studies showed that these two products were the most forgotten items. So yes, it was a cross-sell, designed to add another five dollars to the transaction and ultimately increase profitability, but it also improved the customer experience. Lots of customers would say, "Oh, crap, I almost forgot! Yes, I do need paper." They were happy to be reminded.

With both upselling and cross-selling, the goal isn't to make the customer buy something they don't need; it's to show them something they didn't realize they needed. For instance, if a connoisseur comes in to buy a pre-roll, you could try upselling them to a new infused pre-roll that just came in. That upsell makes sense. You're letting them know about a cool new higher-quality product they might be interested in and weren't aware of before. Essentially, cross-selling is about showing your customers their options.

You could even cross-sell someone like me, a non-cannabis user. While buying cannabis as a gift one day, the sales associate presented me with the option of a THC bath bomb. I don't like getting high, but I do like baths and bath bombs. I was immediately intrigued. Just like with the brisket tacos at Bucc-ee's, I didn't know I needed a THC bath bomb, but it turns out I did. I *loved* it, and I'm delighted the sales associate presented it to me. I've also heard of nicotine-free CBD cigarettes that taste like menthol, with one company trying to match the taste to popular cigarette brands. As someone trying to quit cigarette smoking, that's exactly the kind of thing I would be thrilled to be cross-sold on!

As you upsell and cross-sell, don't be pushy. If someone tells you they have a strict budget or they're clearly in a hurry, don't waste your time and their time trying to force an upsell or cross-sell. For example, last year I needed to buy a new car. I already knew exactly what I wanted—the exact same car I currently had, just the latest model. I showed up at the dealership at eleven o'clock and made it very clear that I had to pick up my daughter at three o'clock. The car salesman I worked with was great. He quickly handled his part of the sale and passed me off to a woman in the finance department, where everything went downhill. She kept trying to upsell me on an extended warranty and tires and a bunch of junk I didn't want. At one point, she pointed her finger in my face and said, "You can wait." Ooh, I saw *red*! I ended up going through with the transaction, after making it clear that I would walk out if she didn't stop, but the customer experience was terrible. I left a review explaining as much, and I don't plan to go back when the time comes to buy my next car.

The Opioid Endemic was caused in part because pharmaceutical companies acted, in my opinion, as drug pushers. We can do better. We *need* to do better. We have a great product with many beneficial uses. We don't need to push it to make more profit. We're not trying to exploit our customers, but to give them the best experience we can. Pushy, high-pressure sales tactics will simply make your customers go elsewhere, but thoughtful upselling and cross-selling, where you present customers with options they're actually interested in, will earn you more customer loyalty.

MEASURE YOUR SERVICE QUALITY

An old saying in business is "What gets measured, gets done." If you want to improve your service quality, you need a way of measuring it.

Start by looking at your customer reviews—on Google, Leafly, Weedmaps, Instagram, and so on. Customers will talk about you everywhere on the internet, and their reviews have a big impact on how other people view you. Look for patterns and trends, both for things you're doing right and things you're doing wrong. Use this information to adjust store policies and coach sales associates on better service.

Take the time to follow up on the bad reviews, because you might be able to turn that poor customer experience into a good one. For example, I once had a frustrating experience with the Cheesecake Factory. My life revolves around being extraordinarily busy, so I wanted to get delivery. However, I had a fifty-dollar gift card and could only use it if I did pickup. Even though it was rush hour, I managed to talk my partner into going to get the food. He goes, gets the food, and heads home, and then the manager calls to inform me that they forgot to give Darrell one of the bags, which happened to contain all the main courses. Coming from a business operations background, I always take the opportunity to not go Karen on a manager, but I do try to provide them with context. I told him that I wouldn't be sending Darrell all the way back to pick up the food because it was too inconvenient. I also explained that because of the COVID-19 pandemic, this was my first time ordering from them in over a year, and they had potentially lost my business because of this poor experience.

I was all ready to never go back again, but then they followed up. The manager refunded the portion of my meal that exceeded my gift card, I got a call from the district manager, and they sent me a hundred-dollar gift card to replace the fifty-dollar gift card I'd used. They completely exceeded my expectations. My family ended up going to the Cheesecake Factory for our first indoor dining room experience postpandemic. We splurged because we had the gift card and had so much fun. It was extra special since it was our first indoor dining experience in so long. If the Cheesecake Factory hadn't followed up, they probably would have lost a customer for life, but because they did, they won me back.

In addition to monitoring customer reviews, you should also conduct customer surveys. I recommend collecting customer emails or phone numbers in order to send out surveys. You could also include survey links at the bottom of the receipt, but since more and more people don't want a receipt or throw it away immediately, I don't recommend it. For surveys to be most effective, you want to get as many responses as possible, so make the surveys convenient and quick to fill out, with only a few questions. Also give customers an incentive to complete the survey, like entering them into a sweepstakes to win a gift card or offering extra points in your loyalty program. As with customer reviews, you want to follow up on any poor customer experiences, so make sure you have some way to contact respondents if necessary.

In addition to looking over customer reviews and surveys on a weekly basis, you should track and monitor a number of service-related metrics, including:

- Average daily transactions (the number of customers you serve in a day)
- Average transaction amount (the total dollar amount of the transaction)
- Average price per item
- Average basket size (the number of items in a transaction)
- Basket mix (the types of items bought together)
- Daily store revenue

These metrics are important because they can give you insights into customer behavior and allow you to forecast trends. For instance, you might find patterns in which types of products are often paired together, which will help you cross-sell more effectively, or you could better plan for a big holiday, like 4/20, by looking at your numbers from the previous year. You can also use these metrics to set goals. Remember, though, that while metrics are important, the customer experience is always more important. You should measure all these things and strive to improve them, but don't put so much pressure on your sales associates that they prioritize meeting their metrics over meeting the customer's needs. The point of measuring these things is to provide better service, not meet arbitrary numbers.

The better you understand the strengths and weaknesses in your service, the more you'll be able to improve, so be sure to track your service through reviews, surveys, and metrics.

Three Quick-and-Dirty Tips
for Excellent Service

1. **Dress the part.** Suits and ties don't make sense for the cannabis industry, but you do need a uniform of some kind. A uniform will make your staff easy to identify and make your store look more professional. The uniform can be as simple as jeans and a company T-shirt you provide.

2. **Host an event.** To really stand out from the competition, get creative and host a special event. It doesn't need to be a huge undertaking. Maybe you have a grower or manufacturer set up a booth in the store to talk about their products, paired with a discount. You could offer cannabis classes for customers who are interested in learning more about certain topics. Maybe you designate senior hours in which you have extra staff to accommodate the special needs of seniors. Perhaps you even coordinate with a local senior center to have a bus stop at your store during those hours.

3. **Create cheat sheets for sales associates.** Sales associates have to remember a lot of information to be effective at their jobs. With time and training, they'll learn what they need to know, but especially while new and in training, cheat sheets are helpful. You could have cheat sheets on the different terpenes, the promotions you're currently running, product recommendations for various customer needs, and more.

EQUIP YOUR SALES ASSOCIATES WITH
THE TOOLS FOR SUCCESS

Remember that everything about the customer experience comes back to leadership. While your sales associates will be the ones to implement the best practices of this chapter, it's *your* responsibility to equip them with the training and education to do so. Part of that will be done during initial onboarding for your sales associates, but training needs to be continuous. You should hold daily standup meetings in which you can communicate current promotions and run through quick refreshers and role-play exercises. On the floor, make sure to reinforce positive behavior and coach sales associates through mistakes or tough situations.

Right now, our product basically sells itself, but with growing competition, your service will become more and more critical. If you don't put effort into this, other retailers will, and they'll take your business. What's more, we have a responsibility as retailers to educate our customers. From the novice users to the connoisseurs, we can break the stigmas and create a delightful customer experience by building trust and providing expert advice.

In my opinion, service is one of the coolest parts of our job. We have an amazing product that people want, and through service, we can solve customer problems and make people happy. No one's going to remember what they bought from you, but they will remember how you made them feel. With delightful service, you can create a feeling such that, if given the chance, the customer will return to you.

Chapter 7

MERCHANDISING

I love Target. They are one of the merchandising masters of the traditional retail world. I can walk into a Target to get towels and end up walking out with towels plus a matching shower curtain, new soap dispenser, snacks, dog toys, and a number of other odds and ends. Through the sheer power of merchandising, Target can turn a planned $50 shopping trip into a $500 one.

This is in large part because Target excels at the two major components of merchandising we'll discuss in this chapter: product selection and product display. In terms of product selection, they've found the profitable middle ground between affordability and quality, offering cheap but chic products. They've thought of everything you might need for your home and daily life and brought it together in one place.

Their product display is particularly impressive to me. You can see thoughtful merchandising decisions all over the store, starting from the moment you first walk in and hit the Dollar Spot section filled with seasonal offerings and cute knick knacks. It draws you in right away and is typically right by the registers, so that you'll be tempted to swing by before checkout too. In the home goods section, you'll find a staged area that shows off furniture, rugs, decorations, and more. By laying everything out, Target helps you visualize what these items would look like in your home and evokes certain feelings, like comfort and warmth. In the makeup section, they have good lighting and mirrors, and everything is designed to make you feel beautiful. The products are also organized so that everything is approximately eye level or below for the average-height woman. (As a shorter woman, I've run into problems in drugstores with makeup being above my head and difficult to reach.)

As you walk through each section of Target, you can notice the ways in which the merchandising is geared toward a certain type of customer. Menswear looks a bit different from womenswear, the toys section is built with kids and parents in mind, and so on. They create mini customer experiences inside of the store while still tying everything together with the larger Target brand, creating a seamless transition from one department to the next.

As retail giants like Target show us, your products and how you present them are a critical part of the customer experience. Rather than just putting anything on the shelf, you need to curate your assortment and organize it in a way that allows customers to easily find what they want and also discover those things they didn't realize they needed until they set eyes on them.

THE POWER OF MERCHANDISING

Merchandising is critical because of one pure and simple truth: if you don't have the best products, people will not come to your store. We're retailers. Our businesses literally cannot exist without our products. Simply having the best products isn't enough either. They need to *look* like the best products, which means how we display them matters too. Just consider the difference between throwing a pile of shirts in a bin versus placing them on hangers and styling a mannequin. Even if the shirts are of the exact same quality, the ones that are displayed on hangers and the mannequin are going to seem far superior.

Merchandising is also important because your products are a reflection of your store. When you put a product in your store, you're endorsing it. To an extent, this is true of any retailer, but it's doubly true for cannabis retailers because customers rely on us so much for recommendations and expert advice. If you sell a cartridge that has been too diluted or a batch of seedy flower, customers will blame you, not just the product. You're the one who put it in your store, told them it was good, and sold it to them. If you stock poor-quality products, customers will lose trust in you and take their business to another store where they know they will get top-quality products for their money.

Collectively, traditional retailers have thousands of years of merchandising experience. They've been working on product sourcing and presentation since they opened their doors, and I can guarantee you that any major retailer today has an entire department dedicated to merchandising. At Office Depot, merchandising was so important that we literally had an entire store set up inside of a warehouse solely for the purpose of staging. We did research on the effects of different end caps, like their impact on average transaction size, and then we used the fake store to test out different product placements in preparation for big sales, like Black Friday and back-to-school shopping.

For cannabis retailers, merchandising has mostly been an afterthought. In the whirlwind of starting up a business, your first priority is simply getting product on the shelves and selling it. I get it—I've been in that whirlwind, running around with hardly a chance to breathe. As the markets mature, though, thoughtful curation of your product assortment and how you present it to your customers will become more important. So if you haven't thought yet about your merchandising, it's time to start.

CURATE YOUR PRODUCT ASSORTMENT

Traditionally, merchandising refers specifically to the display of products in a store, but for displays to be most effective, you must start with a good product assortment. Since cannabis retailers have a large variety of customers, we must be particularly thoughtful about choosing our products.

Note to Reader

I've written this section from the perspective of being able to stock products from multiple suppliers, but in some states, you may not have much choice available to you. Several states have strict licensing caps, which typically results in low innovation and supply. Other legalities can also limit your choice. In Florida, for instance, the cannabis market is set up to be vertically integrated, with only a handful of licensees. This means that there are few companies to innovate and significant capital expenditures to bring new products to market. As a result, the assortment of products is extremely limited. Eventually, I do believe that all markets will open up, and these principles will serve you well at that point. Until then, just do your best. I also encourage you to contact your legislators so we can start getting these overly restrictive laws changed.

In curating your selection, first and foremost, you must identify quality products. You should have somebody called a *merchant* in the company who specializes in finding, assessing, and choosing products. The merchant should have an understanding of both industry-wide and store-specific trends in purchasing behavior. They should also be able to examine flower and determine the quality of the buds, based on appearance and aroma. They should be familiar with various cannabis "stats" (like THCA, THCB, and CBD percentages) and should be able to read and interpret ingredient lists for edible products. Finally, the merchant needs to have a basic understanding of labeling requirements and common lab testing procedures so they can assure the safety of the chosen products.

In addition to checking product quality during the selection process, you should also perform quality assessment checks of individual shipments. Especially with flower, the quality can vary from shipment to shipment, and you don't want to accidentally put a bad batch on your shelves.

After quality, you want *variety*, in five main areas:

1. **Product type.** Different customers like to consume cannabis in different ways, so you want all the major product types covered: flower, pre-rolls, vape cartridges, concentrates, topicals, edibles, and tinctures. Within these large categories, you can typically break things down even further. For instance, within edibles, you may want to stock fruit-based products, chocolate products, beverages, capsules, and oils that can be used for baking.
2. **Strains.** At the most basic level, you need sativas, indicas, and hybrids. On a fine-tuned level, you want to offer different terpene profiles and THC/CBD strengths and have a good selection of popular strains, like Blue Dream and OG Kush.

3. **Price.** Your customers will have different budgets. Some will be bargain hunters, while others are willing to spend the big bucks in order to get uber high-quality products. To serve them all, you'll need a variety of price points.

4. **Product size.** For some product types, like vape cartridges, sizing is fairly standard, but other cannabis products come in a variety of sizes. For flower in particular, you should stock a selection of sizes, from one gram to one ounce, so that you can serve both casual users and bulk buyers.

5. **Target customer.** As mentioned in the branding chapter, while your store should probably have an inclusive brand, individual cannabis products can be more targeted with their branding. To better serve niche customer groups, try to stock a variety of these targeted products. Put yourself in the shoes of various customers—college-aged men, elderly users, professional women, and so on—and ask yourself, "Do I have products that will appeal to this customer?"

As you select products for your store, remember that this is one of your big opportunities to contribute to social equity in the cannabis space. Search for minority-owned suppliers and stock their products. Minority owners face a lot of challenges and barriers to success in our industry. Giving them shelf space is an easy way for you to uplift them and help shrink those barriers a little bit.

ORGANIZE IN A WAY THAT MAKES SENSE

Once you have a high-quality, varied product assortment, you want to present your products in a logical way that takes the customer through the shopping experience. I have found that the two most popular organization methods are by product type and user experience.

One of the best examples of merchandising I've seen in the cannabis space took the latter approach. They set their store up like a rainbow, with each color linked to a particular user experience—for example, blue for sleepy time and yellow for energy. Each section was uniquely designed to evoke the emotions of the experience. Aesthetically, it was incredibly beautiful, and I found that method of browsing delightful. Plus, displaying multiple product types in each color category made it easy to cross-sell.

Organizing by product type also makes sense because many customers come in looking for a particular consumption method. If you organize by product type, you'll have a section for flower, a section for vaping, a section for edibles, and so on. With this organization, customers can easily see and compare their options. If they want to buy multiple products of the same type but with different experiences, everything will be in one place.

Logistically, organizing by product type is usually easier than by experience. Sometimes suppliers will provide you information on the predicted experience for a product, but many times, you'll have to determine this on your own, based on the strain and terpenes. In contrast, to organize by product type all you have to do is look at the product, and you can say, "Yup, that's a pre-roll," and you'll know exactly where it goes. However, if you do the work of organizing by experience in your merchandising, you can make your sales associates' jobs easier. Unless you organize by experience, most customers won't be able to identify which products will give them their desired user experience, and so they will have to rely on sales associates to tell them.

Ultimately, either one of these strategies can be effective. You also might choose an entirely different method of organization. For instance, maybe you want to organize by supplier or by the customer's experience level, with a section for novices and a section for connoisseurs. Perhaps you have an on-site bakery that you want to make the star of the show. As long as the organization is logical, you have some flexibility here. Use your brand to guide your decision.

Once you have an overall method of organization, think about how products are displayed within each section. Does it look cluttered? Is the spacing even? If you're using wall hooks, do you have nice straight lines? Is there a logical flow within each section—for instance, do you group products by supplier, by size, by strain?

Be sure to consider the laws in your state. In some places, you're required to lock your inventory into a vault every night, which means you have to re-merchandise every single day. In this case, you'll want to choose an organization that is quick and easy to implement, and you will need clear maps (or planograms, which we'll discuss in a moment) so that your employees can re-create it the same way each day. Otherwise, you're going to annoy customers who come in and can't find their favorite products because everything's been moved.

Also, think about your store environment. Perhaps you're in a high-crime area and need to keep your product under lock and key, or your store has so much traffic that products fly off the shelves faster than you can restock them. How will you adjust your merchandising? Maybe you use digital menus, in which case you still need to think about how your products are organized and displayed on the screen. Another option is to display fake products or test samples in glass cases and pull from the back inventory when customers make a purchase.

Once you've figured out your layout and organization, you should create a *planogram*. A planogram is a visual map for how to present your products. Planograms can range from a hand-drawn sketch to a highly detailed map created with planogramming software in which exact product dimensions are taken into account and everything is represented to scale. If you have a single store, you can sketch out your merchandising displays on paper, and when adjustments are needed, you can simply rearrange and shift products around. The more stores you have, the more important planograms are to ensure consistency across each store. If your merchandising is inconsistent across locations, customers will struggle to find the products they want, which is frustrating. Planogramming software becomes more useful with more stores, especially if your stores are different sizes or have different floor plans.

Ultimately, there are no one-size-fits-all solutions to merchandising. Seek to make your merchandising reflect your brand, and experiment a bit to figure out what works for your store and customer base.

CHOOSE YOUR SUPPLIERS WELL AND BUILD STRONG RELATIONSHIPS

Your vendors have a big impact not only on your product assortment but also on your product displays. To be most effective in your merchandising, you need to choose reliable suppliers and build solid relationships with them.

Think about a product you love and buy on a regular basis—maybe a breakfast sandwich from your favorite coffee shop, your dog's food, or even a certain brand of toilet paper. Now imagine you make a special trip to the store to pick up this item, and they're out of stock. Not a very fun customer experience, right? You want to avoid that happening in your store, so when choosing products, you need to think about the supplier in addition to the product itself. This is particularly important for your bestselling items. Say Cherry Garcia vape cartridges are your top seller. When you run out and order more, will your vendor be able to fulfill the order in a timely manner? If not, you can still work with that supplier if you think their product is worth it, but you at least need to look for another vendor that offers Cherry Garcia cartridges (or a close alternative) so you can avoid running out of stock.

In some states, retailers do their own packaging on site, but in many cases, suppliers are in charge of their own packaging, which will obviously impact how you're able to display products. Perhaps all your flower suppliers use jars for their packaging, except for *one* supplier who uses hanging pouches. For the sake of your merchandising, you might need to drop that one supplier, or you'll need to figure out how to display the hanging pouches alongside your jars in a way that makes sense. You also have to consider the appearance of the packaging and whether it fits with your brand. A supplier might have a great product, but if it's packaged in a cheap-looking bag, customers aren't going to want it, and your brand could be damaged by association.

If you build good relationships with your vendors, you'll be better able to negotiate with them when needed. Price is an obvious potential negotiation point, but there are other examples too. Perhaps you work out an agreement to have an exclusive launch of an innovative new product, or maybe you can convince a supplier to start doing terpene testing for their products. Maybe you have several suppliers who use hanging pouches for their packaging, and one of them just changed their package width from three inches to five, which has thrown off your entire hanging display. If you already have a good relationship established with them, you might be able to convince them to return to the previous packaging.

This advice comes with a big caveat: for negotiations like this to work, you need to be in a freer market, with multiple potential suppliers. If you're in a state with strict license caps, your hands are tied—you have to take what product you can get, and you're not going to have much, if any, negotiating power with your suppliers. Arguably, that means it's even more important for you to build strong relationships with your suppliers, since you depend so heavily on them. If you are in a market that is heavily capped on the number of licensees, be sure to write your state legislators about the benefits of opening up licenses to make product assortment more accessible.

Five Quick-and-Dirty Merchandising Tips

1. **Highlight your top sellers.** You should know the bestselling products in your store, in each category. Display them prominently, and work with suppliers to ensure you never run out of stock.

2. **Put logical add-ons at the cash wrap.** Think about what customers need but often forget, and what small items make sense to add on to a purchase. Some good examples are lighters, rolling papers, screens, grinders, and pre-rolls. In addition to placing items like this on the counter next to your registers, also consider creating displays by your line, so customers can browse while they wait to check out.

3. **Create a rotating display.** If you often get new products, want to highlight different growers from week to week, or push seasonal offerings, a rotating display is a good solution. This way customers will know where to go to see what's new or currently on special.

4. **Figure out how you're going to communicate your prices.** Some stores don't put prices on their products at all, and, instead, the sales associates communicate this information. Some put price tags on each individual product, some use digital price tags at the front of a shelf, and some even group their products so an entire case is all a single price. To pick your pricing method, consider the price sensitivity of your customers. Customers who care a lot about price will want to see the prices. Also think about how often you will need to adjust prices. If it's frequently, you probably don't want to price each product individually.

5. **Prepare for inventory audits.** Every state has rules about how often you must conduct inventory audits, so plan ahead and merchandise your products in a way that will allow for easy inventory counts. For instance, if you have the same product in five different places in your store, that will make taking inventory more difficult for you because your associates must find all five places to count the inventory accurately.

CONSTANTLY REFINE YOUR MERCHANDISING

Merchandising is not a one-and-done activity. The innovation in our industry is truly out of control (at least in those states without strict license caps), which is amazing. All the innovation means growth opportunities and the potential for big profits. To capitalize on that innovation, though, you need to be constantly adapting and adjusting.

Keep an eye on industry trends so you can forecast and plan for changes in merchandising. For instance, if you opened your store several years ago, you might not have put in a beverage cooler. Today, beverages are more popular, which means you need to think about purchasing a cooler and finding a place for it in your store.

Also be aware of your store's sales trends. The better you get to know your customers and their purchasing behavior, the better you'll be able to tailor your merchandising. Maybe your store is in a wealthier neighborhood and your top-shelf products are selling more than the budget products, or perhaps customers have been raving about a certain item in their reviews. You'll want to adjust your merchandising to reflect those trends.

The retailers who can continuously curate their product assortment and display it with the customer in mind will increase their longevity in the market. So however you choose to merchandise, do it with intention, be logical, and adapt based on trends.

Chapter 8

OMNICHANNEL

B lack Friday. Two words that can simultaneously strike fear and excitement into the hearts of retailers everywhere. Black Friday has earned its reputation as the biggest shopping day of the year. However, I'd argue that Black Friday in the traditional sense is dying, because in-store shopping is being replaced by online purchasing. In 2020, the number of online-only shoppers over Black Friday weekend increased by 44 percent.[77] Obviously, the COVID-19 pandemic likely influenced this increase, but it's part of a larger trend.

This trend has made the implementation of omnichannel strategies a necessity for retailers. Omnichannel is about providing a seamless, excellent customer experience across all the possible shopping channels, whether a customer goes into a store or orders online for delivery or pickup. For

---

[77] Danielle Inman, "Holiday Shoppers Take Advantage of Early, Thanksgiving Weekend Deals," NRF (National Retail Federation), December 1, 2020, https://nrf.com/media-center/press-releases /holiday-shoppers-take-advantage-early-thanksgiving-weekend-deals.

cannabis retailers in particular, doing omnichannel well is a great way to stand out from the competition.

One of the last big projects I spearheaded before leaving Office Depot had to do with both Black Friday and omnichannel. It was a large-scale in-store pickup event to drive sales and foot traffic for Office Depot's Black Friday promotions. That year, based on changes in the market, we foresaw a large shift in customer buying behaviors: customers wanted to shop at home and pick up their merchandise at their leisure. In-store pickup has now become an industry standard, but at the time, there were internal doubts that consumer buying behaviors, especially on Black Friday, would shift away from traditional lines forming outside of the store to traffic driven primarily from online sales. Still, we wanted to be prepared.

We knew that for a large Black Friday in-store pickup event to succeed, the online experience had to be supplemented with effective store operations, which meant paying special attention to our in-store customer pickup experience. While many retailers make the pickup experience appear seamless (which is the goal), without proper planning, a sudden increase in online order volume could have easily created a disastrous customer experience. We could have been overwhelmed by the number of orders to be filled, run into issues due to inaccurate inventory numbers, or failed to provide pickup customers the same level of warm, professional service expected of sales associates.

In preparing for Black Friday, we thus had to plan every aspect of the customer experience. All departments in the company were involved, including but not limited to eCommerce, IT, Merchandising, Visual Merchandising, Pricing, Inventory Management, and Store Operations. We planned everything—the timing of email blasts, pricing strategies, inventory management synced with when orders were placed on the website, and then ultimately the fulfillment in the store, which required new processes to ensure that inventory was properly set aside for customers. As part of this planning, to ensure all sales associates were prepared for the event, the Communications Department created both printed and video training materials.

Ultimately, our planning paid off, and the Black Friday in-store pickup event yielded record-breaking sales, driving substantial foot traffic to the store. If it weren't for the in-store pickup sales, we would not have reached our sales goals that year. Most importantly, customers loved the convenience of finding their deals online. While many people enjoy the thrill of waiting in line on Black Friday, there are plenty of shoppers who just want great deals and have become accustomed to finding those deals from the luxury of their home computer or mobile device. If they can go online, get the deal, and do pickup without having to fight through the crowds, it's an incredibly delightful experience.

This is what omnichannel is all about—providing a consistently great customer experience across all channels of your stores.

WHAT IS OMNICHANNEL, AND WHY DOES IT MATTER?

Omnichannel is the skill and art of aligning your retail store experience and your online web presence. From the customer perspective, your website is not any different from your brick-and-mortar location—it's all the same store and same brand. However, from a staffing perspective, the teams who manage the online experience and the in-store experience are often different. Therefore, a concerted effort is required to make sure those teams are working together. Your job as a retailer then is to create a seamless customer experience, whether a customer is shopping at your physical store, online, or both. I spent much of my corporate career specializing in omnichannel, and I believe it is one of the most important concepts in retail.

The customer's shopping experience usually begins online. According to research from Salesforce, *a whopping 87 percent of customers start their shopping journey online.*[78] Particularly in the cannabis industry, considering the stigma and the newness of the market, it makes sense that most customers' first introduction to your company will come digitally. Imagine cannabis has just been legalized recreationally in your state, and you can't wait to visit a dispensary. You don't yet know what dispensaries are available in your location, so what are you going to do? Google it. Now let's say you're a novice user. A friend recommended a dispensary to you, but you're nervous about going in for the first time. What are you going to do? Google it and check out the dispensary's website. Maybe you're tired of the products you want being out of stock at your usual cannabis store. How will you choose a different store to visit? You know the answer: google it.

Since so many customers start their buying process online, doing omnichannel well translates to increased foot traffic to your store, which means increased in-store sales. Plus, you must consider the potential for online sales. E-commerce has been steadily growing for years now. Customers like the comfort and convenience of shopping from their home. As cannabis retailers, we may be restricted by various laws, but in many states, you can offer your customers pickup and even delivery options. If you're thoughtful about your omnichannel strategy and create a robust, easy-to-use online ordering system, you can stand out from the competition and delight your customers.

---

[78] Heike Young, "Nine Stats About the Retail Customer Journey in 2019," *360 Blog*, Salesforce, April 9, 2019, https://www.salesforce.com/blog/customer-retail-statistics/.

The COVID-19 pandemic further solidified the need for omnichannel retail. As soon as shutdowns and store closures began to sweep across the nation, omnichannel went from nice-to-have to must-have. For many businesses, omnichannel solutions, like delivery and pickup, were the only way to survive. Many states designated cannabis stores as an essential service, so dispensaries were able to continue in-store shopping. Still, many customers preferred not to shop in-store, which meant that the retailers who offered pickup and delivery had a leg up on those who didn't. We never know exactly what the future will hold, but having multiple shopping options gives you greater flexibility and potential to adapt. In any case, global pandemics aside, customers now *expect* to have the option of pickup or delivery.

Still not convinced of how important omnichannel is? Flowhub, one of the top cannabis software companies, found that cannabis stores that allowed customers to order ahead sold 22 percent more on average compared to stores without this capability.[79] Plus, take a look at these overall shopping stats from McKinsey & Company:[80]

- Online sales increased at a 14 percent compounded annual growth rate from 2016 to 2020.
- Buy online, pick up in-store (BOPIS) grew 28 percent year-over-year from February 2019 to February 2020.
- About 22 percent of customers are using delivery services more than before the pandemic.

---

[79] Flowhub, "Cannabis Industry Statistics 2021," accessed July 3, 2021, https://flowhub.com/cannabis-industry-statistics.

[80] Holly Briedis et al., "Adapting to the Next Normal in Retail: The Customer Experience Imperative," McKinsey & Company, May 14, 2020, https://www.mckinsey.com/industries/retail/our-insights/adapting-to-the-next-normal-in-retail-the-customer-experience-imperative.

- 56 percent of consumers report they intend to continue using BOPIS after the pandemic.

Obviously, omnichannel is very important. It can also be very challenging, so here are some tips for success.

DESIGN A GREAT WEBSITE

While it may seem obvious, in the digital era, your company website is the foundation of your online customer experience. It represents your store in the digital world and is likely your customer's first introduction to your brand. We've all spent enough time on the internet to understand that a website can heavily influence one's view of a company. Your first priority in an omnichannel strategy is to ensure your website is sending the message you want.

One of the best things you can do to design a better website is visit the websites of successful cannabis retailers, particularly those in more mature markets, like California, Colorado, and Washington. Beyond that, your website should convey your brand, educate customers, and provide a good user experience. Some of the following advice may seem elementary, but you'd be surprised how often these things are overlooked, especially in the early startup days. By creating a strategic effort around your website, you can generate more online revenue and increase foot traffic to your store.

Convey Your Brand

When someone visits your website, they should immediately get an impression of your brand. The colors, the font, and the images should all support your brand identity. Whether your customer walks into your physical location or opens up your home page online, you want to evoke the same feelings.

Part of conveying your brand means making your purpose clear. You should have an About page that explains your mission and values as well as your story as a company. Sometimes people ask me, "What if I don't have a story?" My answer is usually, "You do." Your story is simply an explanation of why you do what you do and all the work you've done to get to where you are today. What problem does your store seek to solve? What challenges have you faced and overcome? What do you hope to accomplish in the future? That's your story.

Also consider including photos of your store and staff somewhere on your website. This will give customers a feel for your in-store experience and put a face on the business. Especially for customers who are nervous about buying cannabis, a friendly, smiling face on your website can go a long way. To feel authentic, these images should be real photos, not stock images.

If you run separate medical and recreational stores, I recommend having distinct websites for each, though they can be linked to each other. Medical and recreational users typically have different needs, questions, and concerns, and having separate websites allows you to speak very specifically to each and develop a dual brand identity.

Educate Customers

A key component of the in-store customer experience is the education sales associates can provide. To have a seamless omnichannel experience, you need to offer a similar level of education on your website. Many customers, particularly novice users, prefer to get information about cannabis online, from the comfort of their own home, where no one can judge them for their questions or lack of knowledge.

You can start with an FAQ page, most likely divided into two sections: questions about cannabis (like "What's the difference between indica and sativa?" and "What are THC and CBD?") and store-specific questions (like "Do you have a loyalty program?" and "What forms of payment do you accept?"). If you're not sure what questions to include, ask your sales associates what questions they get the most. Ideally, you want all the questions to fit on the screen without needing to scroll very much. If the FAQ is getting too long, you can break it up into separate pages. For instance, maybe you have a "First-Time Visit" page or a "Cannabis Basics" page.

I highly suggest having a blog as well. At the minimum, I recommend creating blog posts for all the basics. Once you've been in the cannabis industry for a while, you spend so much time surrounded by people knowledgeable in cannabis that you forget about the outsiders—the people who haven't used cannabis and don't have any baseline knowledge. Our job is to pull those outsiders along with us, and we do that through education. It might feel silly to write a blog post explaining the difference between cannabis and hemp, but there's someone out there who still needs to hear that. As an added benefit, blog posts can drive traffic to your website. Plus, after going through the basics, you can use your blog to highlight new products or promotions. Build your blog library over time so you don't burn yourself out, and to make it most effective, ensure customers can easily search for and find the specific topics they're interested in.

As you create content, design it to be scannable. Use shorter paragraphs to avoid walls of text that will make readers' eyes glaze over. You can further break up the text and improve readability with headings, graphics, and bulleted or numbered lists. Also use bold or italics to highlight key ideas.

Finally, for medical dispensaries in particular, I also recommend including a chat feature or a dedicated customer service line on the website.

Recreational users often have similar questions to each other, so you can create a single set of educational materials that provide all or most of the answers they need. Medical patients, on the other hand, often have very specific questions that require a one-on-one conversation.

Consider the User Experience

Last but not least, your website needs to function flawlessly and be enjoyable to use. Your website user experience (UX) is often the start of the customer journey, so you want to make a good impression. If the UX is poor, users will leave the website, and you'll lose the chance to convert them into customers.

Start by assessing your website's functionality. Functionality is critical not only to the UX but also to your search engine optimization (SEO), which is the process of designing your site so it appears high in search results, improving the quality and quantity of your web traffic. SEO is about a lot more than just keywords. Broken links, slow load speeds, and other functionality issues will hurt your SEO and make it more difficult for users to find your website. Before you launch your website and anytime you make substantial updates, check for broken links, review the site's appearance in multiple browsers and from different devices (computer, smartphone, tablet, etc.), and ensure images are clear and not grainy. Also make sure your pages load *fast*, including on mobile devices. A Google study found that 70 percent of mobile landing pages took *seven or more* seconds to fully load, with an average load time of fifteen seconds![81] More than 50 percent of web traffic nowadays comes from mobile, and as load time increases from one second to ten seconds, the probability of a user bouncing (leaving the

---

[81] Daniel An, "Find Out How You Stack Up to New Industry Benchmarks for Mobile Page Speed," Think with Google, February 2018, https://www.thinkwithgoogle.com/marketing-strategies/app-and-mobile/mobile-page-speed-new-industry-benchmarks/.

website without looking at other pages or performing the action you want) increases 123 percent.[82] So this is a huge opportunity for you to stand out from the competition. Google's best practice recommendation is a load time under three seconds.[83]

After functionality, consider aesthetics. You should be using *responsive web design*, which means your website automatically adapts based on how it's being viewed—on a desktop, smartphone, tablet, or so on. This will ensure your website looks good, no matter the device. Try to keep the look of the website simple, with good use of negative space and legible fonts. What makes a beautiful website is *clarity*, so don't overcrowd your web pages or use distracting, unclear fonts. In general, avoid doing anything that will distract the user—that means no auto-playing video or sound and no excessive pop-ups. (Minimal pop-up use is okay, like to confirm a user is twenty-one or older or to encourage signing up for your email list.)

The last major component to consider is navigation. The user should be able to find all the information they want and move from place to place on your website with ease. This is key to *conversion rates*, which means the user does something you want them to do—like sign up for your email list, place an online order, and so on. The user should never have to guess or search for the next thing to do. Take the time to plan out your sitemap and think about how you want customers to flow through the website, just as you would think about the flow in your store. Keep in mind that not all customers will come through the "front door," or home page. If they first enter your website through, say, a blog article, you still want to guide them and try to convert them into a customer.

---

[82] Ibid.

[83] Ibid.

Even if you think you've designed a great website, don't assume it's performing as it should. Track and monitor key metrics, like bounce rate and conversion rates. Other helpful metrics are website traffic (how many people visit your site), session duration (how long users spend on the website), and traffic source (how people get to your site—email link, Google search, etc.).

A beautiful, functional website that conveys your brand and educates customers is a great starting point, and it's a largely one-and-done task, which means a one-time upfront investment in your website can pay off for years. The next goal is an online ordering system.

IMPROVE YOUR ONLINE ORDERING EXPERIENCE

If you don't offer online ordering for pickup or delivery, you're losing revenue, pure and simple. In my opinion, every cannabis retailer should have an online ordering system or a plan to create one.

Unfortunately, in some states, it is not legally allowed to offer pickup or delivery. Not only does this harm your customer experience and business, but I would argue that it also deprives your community of a public service. Imagine an immunocompromised individual using cannabis for pain management. If your state does not allow pickup or delivery, that person has to either risk contracting an illness that could kill them or suffer through their pain. As members of the cannabis industry, we have a responsibility to advocate for our customers and raise concerns like this to our local and state legislators. So if you cannot currently offer pickup and delivery, (1) try to change that and (2) have an omnichannel plan ready so you can be ahead of the curve once the laws change. (Given the popularity and consumer demand for pickup and delivery, I do believe these laws are likely to change in the near future.)

For those retailers who are currently allowed to do pickup or delivery, understand that not all online ordering systems are created equal. If your online ordering process is frustrating and confusing, you're hurting your customer experience. To be most effective, your online ordering experience should replicate your in-store experience as much as possible. To that end, here are some suggestions.

Include Product Descriptions and Images

In-store, your customers have the chance to see all your products and get descriptions from your sales associates, so you need to include that information online as well.

A lack of images and robust product descriptions is the number one mistake I see cannabis retailers make when it comes to online ordering. Some stores don't include any description at all beyond the name of the product. Others only indicate the product type (flower, concentrate, etc.) and perhaps categorize it as sativa-dominant or indica-dominant. If you look at major retailers outside of the cannabis industry, you'll see a vast difference. Traditional retailers understand that if a customer is going to buy something, they want to know exactly what they're buying. You can go to Target.com, look up a bag of shredded cheese, and find a better, more detailed product description than most cannabis retailers provide. And unlike cheese, you can get vastly different user experiences from cannabis products, which means product descriptions are arguably far more important for us.

You should have a professional image that properly depicts each product in your online store, and a description that includes as much information as possible. This should include: the ingestion method, THC and CBD percentages, strain and terpene information, expected user experience, and, when relevant, ingredient list.

Adding an image and description for a single product is easy enough, but once you multiply it by the hundreds of products you may stock, this task can feel overwhelming. The trick to making it manageable is to get the images and descriptions from the suppliers. Office Depot's website includes lots of great images and descriptions for its products, from pens all the way up to office chairs and computers. Do you think Office Depot took all those pictures and wrote the descriptions? Heck no! The companies who manufacture the products provide most of the data, then a third party assists with augmenting it for SEO purposes. As part of the negotiation with suppliers, your merchant should request product images and descriptions. Really, providing these digital assets is in the supplier's best interest, as customers are naturally more drawn to products with an image and description.

Even with supplier-provided digital assets, adding this information to your online ordering system can be a monumental task. You need to review everything before posting it, as anything you include on your website is a reflection of you and your brand. Plus, your product assortment probably changes regularly, which means you must continually be updating your website. Considering this, *it is important that you have a team member responsible for this task.* You don't need to upload images and descriptions for every single one of your products at once. To start, do it just for new products as you add them into the system. Then set a goal of doing *x* number each week, focusing on your most popular products first. Over time, you'll slowly build your library of descriptions and images.

Create Filters for Easy Sorting

Because cannabis stores often stock a *lot* of different products, giving customers a way to sort and filter through their options is critical. You should categorize products so that your online store reflects the merchandising of your physical location, whether that means organizing by product type, expected user experience, or something else.

Matching your overall merchandising strategy is the minimum for filtering options. One of the beauties of online stores is that you can reorganize all the products with just a few clicks, so you're not locked into a single organization method. In-store, sales associates help to narrow a customer's options. Online, filters must do this work. So ideally, you will include a variety of filters beyond your primary merchandising strategy. Here are some you may want to include:

- Product type
- Expected user experience
- Indica, sativa, hybrid, or CBD
- Price
- Size
- Brand
- THC or CBD percentage
- Terpene profiles
- Issue-oriented considerations (e.g., minority-owned brands, organic, etc.)

In addition to having filters, you should also allow customers to search for products by keyword and to change the sort method. The most common sorting options are alphabetical, price (both low to high and high to low), popularity, and customer rating.

Set Up a Customer Review System

In my experience, very few cannabis retailers have set up their online stores to allow for product-specific reviews, which means this is a huge opportunity to stand out. Product-specific customer reviews provide customers with real, trustworthy insight into a product. If your customer Dave sees that a product has multiple five-star reviews and that other customers report having the experience he wants, he can feel confident in purchasing it. Essentially, customer reviews can take the place of a sales associate's advice. As a side benefit, enabling product-specific reviews can also help inform your merchandising decisions. If a product is consistently getting one-star reviews, for instance, you know to stop stocking it.

Allowing product-specific reviews is the first step. The next step is actually getting customers to leave reviews. Starting with the order receipt, you can encourage reviews by simply including "Leave a Review" links for each product. Several days after a purchase, once the customer has had a chance to actually use the products, you could send a follow-up email asking them to leave a review to help other customers. You could also offer extra points in your loyalty program in exchange for leaving reviews. Another great incentive is to set the system up so that customers have access to all their own reviews. In this way, leaving reviews can serve as a cannabis experience journal for them. They may want to leave reviews simply so they can keep track of which products they do and don't like.

Also try to make the process of leaving a review as easy as possible for the customer. For instance, you could include lists of user experiences (sleepy, creative, energetic, relaxed, etc.) or common side effects (hungry, dry eyes, etc.) and have customers click the ones they experienced. Not all customers are willing to write a paragraph review, but many will be happy to click a few buttons.

DO PICKUP AND DELIVERY RIGHT

Once a customer places an order, you've made a sale, but the customer experience is far from over. You now need to fulfill that order efficiently and accurately, in alignment with your brand and expected level of service. Pickup and delivery will only have a positive impact on your customer experience if you do them well. If someone orders delivery and the order shows up an hour later than promised, or if they order pickup and then the order isn't ready or is missing items when they arrive, you've created a poor customer experience. So when someone makes an online order, you must have a clear, reliable process in place for how that order will be fulfilled.

Once a customer places a pickup order, who inside the store will be responsible for preparing the order, and how will they be notified of the order? How will you ensure order accuracy? Will the sales associate double-check the order when the customer comes in to pick it up? Will you have a separate pickup line so customers don't have to wait? How will that line be marked so customers know where to go?

For delivery, will you offer a pizza delivery model where you deliver as soon as possible, or will you offer appointment slots? How will you measure whether your drivers are making their deliveries on time? Most states have rules that require your delivery vehicles be GPS equipped. When using GPS, will you have a dispatcher monitoring driver movements to ensure deliveries are happening in a timely manner? What training will you give delivery drivers to ensure they provide excellent service aligned with your brand when they drop the order off? Do your drivers look safe enough to deliver to Grandma? I know that seems silly, and we shouldn't judge people based on appearances, but the reality is that the appearance of your drivers does matter. Will they have a uniform? Will you provide the delivery vehicles? How will you handle insurance? What software will you use to optimize the delivery drivers' routes?

You have lots of questions to consider as you develop your pickup and delivery options. It may feel overwhelming at first, but remember that you can always improve over time. Put the best processes in place that you can to ensure accuracy and efficiency, then pay attention to customer and employee feedback and adjust accordingly.

Four Quick-and-Dirty Omnichannel Tips

1. **Be willing to pay for a website.** If you happen to be an experienced web developer, then great, make your own website! The rest of us need to either hire a professional or, at the very least, use a website-building service. Your website is crucial, so it's worth investing a bit of money into it.

2. **Take professional photos of your store and staff.** Photos are a great way to connect with your customers online and show them who you are as a company. To represent your brand well, those pictures need to be high quality. Think about composition, framing, and lighting. Similar to your website, you might consider investing in a professional photographer. A one-time fee upfront will get you professional photos you can use again and again.

3. **Use e-commerce software.** Obviously, building your own online ordering system from scratch will take a lot of work. Instead, you might consider purchasing an e-commerce software solution. Just make sure it's compatible with your other systems and allows for customization, like adding in product descriptions and images.

4. **Develop your own app.** A good online ordering system should be your first priority, but as you grow and scale, you can consider developing your own mobile app. M-commerce—shopping through a mobile device (primarily smartphones)—has exploded in recent years. Insider Intelligence predicts that m-commerce will make up 44 percent of e-commerce by 2024.[84] Apps tend to provide a much better customer experience than internet browsers on mobile devices, particularly for shopping, so they can take your omnichannel experience to the next level. As an added benefit, you can link your loyalty program (which we'll discuss in Chapter 9) to your app as well.

TAKE IT SLOW AND COORDINATE ACROSS THE COMPANY

You're not going to build a perfect website or create a seamless omnichannel experience overnight, and that's okay. You simply need to get started. Carve out a little time to create an omnichannel plan and then delegate. Put someone in charge of gathering product descriptions from suppliers, another person in charge of writing blogs, and so on.

---

[84] Andrew Meola, "Rise of M-Commerce: Mobile Ecommerce Shopping Stats & Trends in 2021," *Business Insider*, December 30, 2020, https://www.businessinsider.com/mobile-commerce-shopping-trends-stats.

As you work on your omnichannel strategy, my number one tip for success is to communicate and coordinate across the company. Omnichannel is about re-creating your entire in-store customer experience online, and since multiple departments are involved in creating your customer experience, omnichannel efforts require the input and participation of multiple departments. You need a concerted partnership between IT, store operations, merchandising, promotions, supply chain, inventory management, graphic design, and more.

With continuous effort and multidepartment collaboration, over time your customer won't be able to tell the difference between your website presence and your in-store experience. They will be seamlessly integrated, reflecting the same brand and sparking the same feelings of delight.

Chapter 9

MARKETING: PROMOTIONS AND LOYALTY PROGRAMS

I'm a crafter. Crocheting, sewing, painting, creating home decor—I thoroughly enjoy it all. When I have free time on a weekend, I love crafting with my daughter. Nothing is better than custom curtains or pillows for the couch. My outdoor furniture is all refurbished and upcycled with new paint and cushion covers. Naturally, playing into my love for crafty creations, one of my favorite places to shop is Jo-Ann's. Not only does Jo-Ann's carry nearly everything I could ever need to create dazzling gifts and home decor, but I find that their marketing to me is both thoughtful and successful.

Every Sunday morning, around ten o'clock, Jo-Ann's texts me a coupon—a *good* coupon, most often 20 percent off my purchase or 40 percent off a single item. The coupon itself is delightful, but the timing is also important. I'm a busy mom. If I go to Jo-Ann's, it's going to be on the weekend, usually Sunday. If they sent the coupon to me on Tuesday, I'd look at it and immediately forget it, because I have a million other things to do and think about during the week. By sending it to me on Sunday, when I need it and am most likely to use it, they increase both my delight and their chances of actually getting me into the store. They're even smart enough to recognize that I probably sleep in on Sundays, so they should send it to me later in the morning, when I'm up.

Now, do I go to Jo-Ann's every week? No. In fact, I haven't been to the store in close to six months because I'm too busy for crafting projects right now. I don't mind the weekly texts, though, because I know that eventually I'll have more time and will go back to Jo-Ann's. When I do, I know I can count on having coupons. The consistency and reliability of the marketing texts is part of why I'm so loyal to Jo-Ann's. Why would I go to a different craft store when I know I have coupons for Jo-Ann's?

Nowadays, customers have so much choice in the marketplace that marketing is not optional. As more cannabis stores open in your area, I guarantee they will be marketing, and they'll be targeting your customers. To compete, you need to have your own marketing strategy.

THE DUAL PURPOSE OF MARKETING: GENERATE REVENUE AND DELIGHT THE CUSTOMER

Marketing includes everything you do to promote your store and sell your products. Obviously, the purpose of marketing is to generate more revenue, but to do that most effectively, your marketing should have a secondary purpose as well: delighting the customer.

Everywhere you look, you can find advertisements—on TV, in magazines, on social media, in your email inbox, and even on billboards while driving down the road. For your marketing to stand out in this sea of ads, it needs to delight the customer in some way. Smart, funny, or heartwarming advertisements can certainly work. Another good strategy is to alert customers to things they may need or want but don't know about yet. For instance, if Chipotle starts offering a new product, the only way I will know about it as a customer is if they market it. Since I like Chipotle, I'd be delighted to discover they have a new menu item.

Unfortunately, because of the stigma of cannabis, we have a lot of legal restrictions about how and where we can market. For instance, we cannot advertise on television or social media in the same way that traditional retailers can. These restrictions mean we need to be creative in how we market to our customers. Fortunately, two of the most delightful marketing strategies are still available to us: promotions and loyalty programs.

Both of these strategies are important because they can help create customer loyalty. Creating loyalty means creating a customer that wants to give your store money *again*. As a retailer, you can't get a better compliment than that. Customer loyalty is also the best way to ensure long-term profitability. You can assume that, over their lifetime, each of your customers will spend a certain amount of money purchasing cannabis. If you convince a customer to shop with you a single time, you might earn one hundred dollars in revenue. If you can earn their long-term loyalty, they will spend thousands, even tens of thousands, of dollars at your store—that's their customer lifetime value. Gaining the loyalty of any given customer is thus much more valuable than winning a single transaction, especially since acquiring new customers tends to cost significantly more than retaining existing customers.

Ultimately, loyalty pivots on your customer experience, so all the strategies in this book are meant to encourage more customer loyalty. However, with promotions—and, especially, with loyalty programs—you can encourage loyalty more explicitly. Promotions give customers a clear reason to return to your store, and a loyalty program rewards them for repeat purchasing behavior.

So let's take a closer look at how you can market more effectively, with a focus on promotions and loyalty programs.

REACH YOUR AUDIENCE

The first step in marketing is reaching your desired audience. Here, you're trying to reach different segments: new customers, existing customers, and the public at large.

Acquiring new customers is typically the most costly in terms of marketing expense, and it can be especially difficult for cannabis retailers since so many traditional advertising methods are closed to us. Online, the two primary places you can advertise are Weedmaps and Leafly. I know some retailers take issue with these sites because you have to pay a fee to be listed and to advertise on the platform. However, the reality is that they're the industry leaders right now. *Lots* of customers visit these sites, so if you can afford it, I highly recommend using them. You should also work on your SEO (search engine optimization) so that you're one of the top results when customers search for dispensaries in your area. Offline, your primary marketing to new customers will likely be your storefront itself and possibly some billboards. Your storefront should be attractive and welcoming, and your sign should be easily visible from the road. Make sure your storefront and any billboards reflect your branding.

Once a customer walks through your door for the first time, they become an existing customer, and the goal is to retain them. That starts by delighting them with the customer experience, but you also want to market directly to them, which means you need a way to contact them: either an email address or a phone number. Lots of businesses ask for this information at checkout, so customers are used to it and often don't have a problem sharing this information. To further incentivize customers, though, instead of directly asking for an email address or phone number, ask them if they want to sign up for your loyalty program. You will still be gathering their email address or phone number, but this way, customers feel as if they are getting something in return for sharing their contact information. Once you have an email address or phone number, you can send marketing messages directly to your existing customers.

The final aspect of your marketing is about reaching not just potential customers, but the general community, in order to improve their perception of the cannabis industry. A population of people out there still think cannabis—and by extension, cannabis retailers—are "bad." It's like we're covered in this scary black haze that screams, "Danger!" When people are scared of something, it's difficult, but not impossible, to change their minds. To win over the larger public, I strongly believe in community involvement and good old-fashioned face-to-face conversations. When people have prejudices against and misconceptions about cannabis, the best way to break through to them and dispel the haze is to give them a face to the business—a face that is warm and friendly, that answers people's questions, and that makes us seem human instead of scary.

Here are some ideas that will help you reach the public as a whole as well as potential customers:

- Become a member of your local chamber of commerce and either attend meetings yourself or appoint someone in your company to represent you.

- Sponsor and participate in local events. (Be thoughtful about this—a cannabis booth might not be welcome at a farmer's market, where children are present, but could be a good idea for a music festival. Also be aware of legal restrictions. Chances are, you won't be able to sell any product at the booth, but you can hand out business cards and answer people's questions.)
- Partner with local nonprofits.
- Send out press releases, making sure to include information about your store's higher purpose and how you want to give back to the community.
- Get involved in non–cannabis industry organizations, like small business associations and networking groups, and attend mixers.

Once you've figured out a way to reach customers, you need to determine the content of your marketing messages. One of the trickiest aspects of marketing is that it's very easy to annoy customers, and an annoyed customer isn't going to want to buy things from you. Fortunately, there's one thing customers always love: sales. For this reason, promotions should be a core part of your marketing strategy.

Social Media Tips

One of the challenges we face due to cannabis's Schedule I status is limitations on how we can use social media. Most social media platforms have rules prohibiting the promotion of illegal drugs, so if you're not careful, your account will be suspended or deleted. With that in mind, here are some tips for using social media:

- **Make your account private.** A key issue with social media is that you don't want to accidentally advertise to children. If you make your account private, people must request to follow you, and you can ensure that only those who want to see your content do. You can also include a note that following the account is a user's confirmation that they are at least twenty-one years old.
- **Don't try to sell anything.** This is one of the fastest ways to get your account flagged. Don't post prices, advertise sales, or do anything else that could be viewed as selling cannabis.
- **Include a link to your website.** While you shouldn't try to sell anything, you *can* include a link to your website. You're allowed to post prices and promote your products on your website, so this is a helpful loophole.
- **Expect to get your account deleted.** There's a lot of gray area for cannabis companies using social media. Even if you're doing your best to follow the rules, your account might be deactivated. If that happens, you'll lose all your followers. Plan ahead for this possibility by encouraging your followers to sign up for your email or text marketing list. That way, even if your account is deleted, you have another way to contact your followers.

CREATE A PROMOTIONAL CALENDAR

In the traditional retail world, a marketing best practice is to create a promotional calendar. Before the internet, advertising revolved around the Sunday newspaper. As a retailer, you had to get your materials to the printer well ahead of time to make sure your flyers were ready to go come Sunday, so planning was a necessity. Today, we're no longer held to the same strict weekly promotional schedule and have more fluidity. However, if you want your sales to be most effective, you should still take the time to sit down and plan out your promotional calendar. Remember my example about Jo-Ann's: consistency matters. Customers often shop according to a schedule, and if you have a clear, consistent promotional calendar, they'll shop with you more consistently.

One strategy is to adopt regular rotational sales. Maybe concentrates are on sale the first week of the month, then flower the second week, then merchant's choice the third week (where the merchant works with suppliers to choose products to discount), and edibles the fourth week. You could also choose to rotate sales by day of the week, with Monday for oils, Tuesday for pre-rolls, Wednesday for edibles, and so on. Another strategy is to offer special "happy hour" deals, where the deals themselves may change but customers know they can count on *something* being on sale during certain hours.

You should also create a calendar for big holiday sales. You should have sales for the normal big retail holidays, like Black Friday, Christmas, and Valentine's Day. In the cannabis industry, we also have a couple of holidays unique to us: 4/20 and Dab Day (7/10, or *OIL* backward and upside down). There are any number of other holidays you could choose to celebrate with a sale: Mother's Day and Father's Day, Memorial Day, Fourth of July, Oktoberfest, and so on. I know of one successful retailer that doesn't do any sort of weekly sales, but they make sure to have one big holiday sale each month.

Particularly for holiday sales, plan these promotions *well* in advance so you can properly market them as well as work with your vendors to ensure proper stock. According to BDSA, daily sales for 4/20 are typically two to three times higher than normal,[85] so you definitely need to plan ahead to make sure you have enough inventory and sales associates scheduled to work. At Office Depot, we'd start working on our Black Friday ad in August, if not sooner. Cannabis retailers will often look at me funny when I suggest planning for a promotion months ahead of time, but the sooner you start planning, the more control you have. For instance, maybe a pumpkin pie cannabis strain has gotten popular, and you know you want to feature it for your Black Friday sale. If you wait until just a month before Black Friday, *everybody* is going to want the pumpkin pie strain, and you'll struggle to get enough stock. If you go to the cultivator in August, though, you'll have an easier time getting stock, *and* by buying in bulk in advance, you may be able to negotiate a better price on it.

In planning your promotions, you should always have clear goals. Maybe you want to hit a revenue dollar amount, drive a certain amount of foot traffic, or sell x units of a particular product. Whatever your goals, think about the metrics you want to drive and how your promotion can support that. For instance, if you want to drive the total transaction amount, maybe you should offer an increasing discount at different price tiers: 10 percent off a purchase of $50 or more, 15 percent off $75 or more, 20 percent off $100 or more. If you want more cross-category sales long-term, maybe you do a "buy a concentrate, get a pre-roll free" sale in order to introduce customers to a new type of product they don't normally buy. If you want to increase foot traffic during a slow weekday, you could have a regular sale that day, and if you want to drive foot traffic on a big sale weekend, like Black Friday or 4/20, you could run an enticing doorbuster deal. You might even decide to use a loss leader, where you sell a certain product below market cost in

[85] Nielsen, "Winning In-Store."

order to get people into the store, where the assumption is they'll buy other things and make up the loss.

Once you've planned your promotion, you need to tell your customers about it. You could run an incredible sale, but if your customers don't know about it, what's the point? Use the email addresses and phone numbers you've gathered from customers to notify them of the sale. For big sales, you may want to send out a message a week or two in advance so customers know it's coming. Then you can send a second message as a reminder the day of or the day before. Also consider posting flyers in your store and updating your website to advertise the sale so customers who aren't on your marketing list are still aware of it.

As a final tip, keep an eye on what other retailers in your area are doing, but remember that the ultimate goal here is customer loyalty. You don't need to get into an all-out price war and beat your competitors on every promotion. You just need to consistently offer good sales that delight customers and make them want to return.

Four Quick-and-Dirty Marketing Tips

1. **Provide value to the customer.** Work to always be relevant in your marketing messages, focusing on information the customer cares about, like promotions and new products. With each message, ask yourself, "What value does this provide the customer?" If you're only thinking about the value the customer can provide to you, and not the other way around, your marketing won't work.

2. **Don't be a nuisance.** Be thoughtful about how often you send out marketing messages. Sometimes less is more. Consider giving customers

the option to choose how often they want to receive messages. Some customers like getting a weekly email, while others only want one a month. Also be aware of relevant federal and state laws regulating how businesses can communicate with customers, like the Telephone Consumer Protection Act (TCPA). It's easier than you might expect to violate these laws and cross into "spam" territory, which can come with costly consequences.

3. **Get creative with holiday promotions.** When you think about promotions, you probably think about discounted pricing—20 percent off, two for one, five-dollar grams, and so on. It's a great strategy, and one you should use, but also consider how you can create a unique, delightful experience for customers beyond price. For example, what if you created a "spa day" basket for Mother's Day, with some chocolate edibles, a THC bath bomb, and topical lotion? For Christmas, what if you offered free on-site gift wrapping for all purchases over seventy-five dollars? Get creative!

4. **Take advantage of cannabis tourism with thoughtful partnerships.** One interesting side effect of the state-driven legalization of cannabis is the rise of cannabis tourism. Some people will specifically travel to a state for cannabis, and even if it's not the primary motivator for their trip, they're still interested and open to trying it. You can market to these individuals by partnering with tourist-driven businesses, like hotels, tourist guides, taxis and rideshare services, and so on. For instance, I recently went to Las Vegas, and during check-in at my hotel, I was given a card from a dispensary with information about a variety of sampler boxes they offered, with different assortments and price points. They even offered an option to place an order privately and have it delivered directly to your room. Considering people on vacation may

be interested in cannabis, are often willing to splurge a bit, and frequently don't have a car, this dispensary's approach was well thought out and delightful!

OFFER A LOYALTY PROGRAM

Storewide promotions can encourage customer loyalty, but if you really want customers to be dedicated to your store, you should also offer a loyalty program. Loyalty programs are one of the most effective customer retention strategies. Traditional retailers are not nearly as restricted in their marketing content as we are, and even they use loyalty programs extensively. Because of this, customers have come to *expect* loyalty programs. With a loyalty program, customers are directly rewarded for their consistency. The more they shop with you, the more they get in return, typically in the form of discounts or free items. Essentially, a loyalty program makes the act of loyalty itself delightful.

Loyalty programs come in many forms and can be very effective. I personally use several loyalty programs. When I eat at Chipotle, I rack up points that earn me free food. With my Amazon Prime credit card, I get money back to shop on Amazon. The membership club at my grocery store gives me special pricing and personalized coupons. Sometimes a loyalty program is actually my primary reason for spending money with a company. For instance, I've been a Spirit Airlines credit card holder for years. Spirit Airlines is *not* known for a good customer experience, and if I didn't have loyalty points to spend, I would not fly Spirit Airlines nearly as much. I don't like their tiny seats or baggage restrictions, but with the points I earn from their credit card, I can fly basically for free, which is delightful enough to balance out the poor customer experience. After cashing in my points once, I was able to take five girlfriends to Saint Thomas for my birthday for only one hundred dollars!

Aside from encouraging the repeat customer behavior you want, loyalty programs have become standard, so customers expect you to have one. Fortunately, as with much of the advice in this book, you can start small. You don't have to create a perfect, robust loyalty program from the get-go. When you first open, your loyalty program might consist of punch cards. This strategy is easy and cheap to implement. All you need is printed cards to hand out and either a hole punch or a stamp. Customers can get a punch or stamp every time they visit the store or spend x dollars. Then, once a customer fills out their card, they can turn it in for a reward.

As you grow, your loyalty program can get more refined and will likely become a points system. A points system gives you a lot of flexibility because you can reward points for a variety of activities. You could give points for the dollars a customer spends, for leaving product reviews, for posting about you on social media, and so on. You can also offer double points to incentivize certain behavior, like shopping on certain days of the week (when you want to drive more traffic) or buying certain products (when you want to move inventory). In this way, not only will your loyalty program build customer loyalty, but it will also help you build your brand, improve your online shopping experience, and attract more customers!

To use a points system, you need some way to track a customer's purchases. You have two basic strategies: (1) link a customer's purchases to their email or phone number (which means you must ask for this information each time at checkout) or (2) use an app with a QR code that the customer can scan. The first strategy tends to be best for most cannabis retailers. If you have the resources to build your own store app, that's incredible, and I highly recommend it. For most retailers, though, that's a long-term strategic goal for five to ten years down the line. A third strategy is to hand out physical loyalty cards with a barcode, which the customer can keep in their wallet or on their keychain. I only recommend doing this in coordination with the first strategy. Because of the stigma of cannabis, some customers will not want to advertise their cannabis usage with a keychain card, and there's always the possibility of a customer losing or forgetting their card. As long as they can also link their purchases to their loyalty account using a phone number or email address, this is fine.

After determining how to keep track of a customer's purchases, you need to figure out your reward system. Some common loyalty rewards include:

- Percent-off discounts (either of a single product or full purchase)
- Dollar savings or cash back
- BOGO (buy one, get one) coupon
- Free items
- Free delivery

In addition to rewards based on purchasing behavior, some retailers also offer perks simply for being a member of the loyalty program, like early access to sales or new product releases.

In deciding what rewards you're going to use, you need to think about your customers. The reward needs to delight them, and different customer populations may be delighted by different things. For example, I once visited a cannabis store where, on every fifth visit, customers got to spin a prize wheel for a free product. I didn't get to spin the wheel myself since it was my first visit, but just watching someone else spin was a delightful experience for me. A spinning wheel is such a fun idea, but it won't work for every store. This particular store was in a rural location, so they had relatively low foot traffic. In a store that sees over a thousand customers a day, the time needed to spin a wheel simply wouldn't be practical because it would end up slowing down lines and annoying customers.

You also must be aware of potential legal restrictions. Many traditional retailers will give customers a free item as a reward, but in some states, you're not legally allowed to give cannabis away for free, even as part of a loyalty program.

Setting up a good loyalty program is a unique skillset. Personally, I would go right to a loyalty program consultant or use third-party loyalty program software designed specifically for the cannabis space. As long as you are doing something to directly reward customer loyalty, though, you're on the right track.

PAY ATTENTION TO YOUR DATA AND ANALYTICS

For your marketing, promotions, and loyalty program to be most effective, you need to collect and analyze all the data available to you, on both a store and customer level. So much of the customer experience hinges on your relationship with each individual customer, yet you undoubtedly have *many* customers—far more than you can personally connect with. Customer data is how you can create a personalized customer experience and relationship at scale. The best mechanism to track and utilize such data is a customer relationship management (CRM) software. A robust CRM system will allow you to track the journey with a customer and provide a personalized customer experience. For example, my veterinarian sends my dog a birthday card each year. While silly, it makes me happy. Incorporating little things like that into the customer experience, using a CRM system, can increase the number of recurring purchases.

Obviously, the primary benefit of a loyalty program is increased customer loyalty. However, a secondary benefit that should not be overlooked is increased customer data. Once a customer signs up for your loyalty program, you have a way to track their purchasing behavior on a personalized level, which allows you to get to know your customers better. You can learn whether they're male or female, when their birthday is, what products they buy, when they shop, and more. You can use all that information to better understand their wants and needs as customers.

Let's address the elephant in the room: data collection and tracking exist in an ethically gray area. Data collection and tracking cross the line into creepy and unethical when companies have access to data a customer didn't explicitly give to them or when they use data in a predatory way. For instance, if somehow you were able to know when a customer went through a breakup, lost their job, or had a loved one die and then targeted them in this vulnerable moment, that's unethical and will damage your customer experience. On the other hand, using a customer's purchasing history with your store to offer them coupons they actually want is delightful. Yes, ultimately you want to use customer data to increase revenue, but you always have to keep the customer experience in mind.

There are many ways you can use customer data to simultaneously increase revenue and add value to the customer experience:

- **Send more targeted, relevant marketing messages.** While your overall branding message should be inclusive, marketing is an area where you can begin to funnel down and target very specific customer segments. Maybe you identify that some customers buy only concentrates, while other customers buy flower exclusively. Tailoring your marketing messages so that you send concentrates deals to the concentrates customers and flower deals to the flower customers just makes sense. Perhaps you identify another segment of customers as connoisseurs that prefer to buy top-shelf products. You can send them a marketing email about the amazing new Cannabis Cup–winning strains you're stocking. With targeted marketing, you're providing more value to the customer, and you're not wasting your time trying to sell customers something they don't want.

- **Offer better, more personalized rewards.** You can use customer data to offer more personalized, delightful rewards. A customer who regularly orders delivery will be delighted by a free delivery promotion, but a customer who only shops in-store will need a different reward to be delighted.

- **Celebrate special occasions with the customer.** If you gather birthdays as part of your loyalty program, you can send special individualized birthday rewards. You could also send "anniversary" rewards to celebrate how long someone has been a customer. I've even had companies send me Mother's Day rewards because they know I'm a mother. Celebrating with a customer can help you form a more personal connection and make them associate you with happy, joyful moments.

- **Cross-sell and upsell more effectively.** The better you understand what products a customer buys and is interested in, the better, more delightful recommendations you can offer.

- **Regain loyalty.** If a customer used to visit your store every week but hasn't been in for a couple of months, you can send them a "We miss you!" email with a coupon that will delight them to try to win back their loyalty.
- **Send emails and promotions at the right time.** You can use a customer's purchasing history to determine when the best time is to send them emails and coupons. For instance, someone who always comes in on Saturday afternoons should get their coupons on Friday evening or Saturday morning.
- **Plan better from an operations standpoint.** By using loyalty program data to predict customer behavior, you can better manage your inventory and plan for staffing. I used to eat at Chipotle five nights a week, and now I eat there maybe once a week. Chipotle can use that information to better predict how much steak and cheese they need in the store. Better planning means less chance of out-of-stocks, which is good for customers.

In addition to using individualized customer data, you should also use storewide data to assess the effectiveness of and better design your marketing, promotions, and loyalty program.

Know this information for your email or text marketing messages:

- What's your clickthrough rate (the number of customers who click on a link in the message)?
- What's your conversion rate (the number of customers who perform the action you want, like making an online order)?
- How about your forwarding rate?
- And, finally, your unsubscribe rate?

For your promotions, you will want to know:

- Are they profitable?
- Did your chosen sale do what you wanted it to do, like increase store traffic or basket size?
- Did your loss leader attract enough corollary sales to offset the loss?
- How can you better prepare for next year?
- Did you run out of inventory on any product?
- Did the dispensary down the road steal a lot of your traffic because they threw a concert?
- In addition to looking at the metrics, ask staff whether customers seemed delighted. Did any particular deals excite them?

For your loyalty program, understand:

- How many customers are signing up for the program?
- Are they actually using their loyalty rewards?
- Has the introduction of the loyalty program driven more traffic to the store?
- And the biggest question of all: is your loyalty program actually driving more customer loyalty?

Data is a valuable tool for retailers, and you need to be tracking and analyzing key metrics. Make sure, though, that you are using your data to create win-win scenarios: increased revenue for your store and also an improved experience for customers.

BE CREATIVE AND FOCUS ON CUSTOMER LOYALTY

If you're the only shop in town right now, you might not have to worry much about marketing, promotions, and loyalty programs, but someday, you're going to have competition. Marketing is what will keep you relevant, by walking the fine line between reminding your customers what you offer, while simultaneously anticipating what will delight them.

Although the legal restrictions we must operate under while marketing can be annoying and frustrating, necessity is the mother of invention. Get creative with your marketing. Embrace the challenges, because they are what will lead you to coming up with cool, innovative ideas that delight customers.

Throughout your marketing efforts, keep your focus on the customer experience. Shift your focus from encouraging individual sales to earning long-term customer loyalty. A customer's true value is how much they will spend at your store over their entire lifetime, not how much they spend in any one transaction. Every time a customer chooses to spend their money with you, you should feel honored. They have other choices, but they chose *you*. You should cherish and reward that loyalty with a loyalty program, delightful promotions, and marketing that adds value to the customer experience.

Chapter 10

STORE OPERATIONS

W hen I think operations, I think NASCAR. On the surface, NASCAR racing can seem deceptively simple. The driver goes around the same track again and again, periodically stopping to refuel and change tires. You've probably driven a car before, gotten gas, and even changed a tire. The tasks themselves are fairly easy. What's difficult is doing these tasks *perfectly*, every single time.

My favorite NASCAR driver was Tony Stewart, partly because he used to drive the Office Depot car. While Stewart was the one I cheered for, he didn't win races alone. It's a good metaphor for a retail store. The driver is the face of the operations, like your front-of-house sales associates. To win races, Stewart had to hit every turn just right, strategize passing, make adjustments based on the changing weight of the car as fuel was used, and more—all at speeds over two hundred miles per hour. Similarly, your sales associates need to provide exceptional service every time, adapting based on each individual customer.

Yet to succeed, Stewart needed an entire team, also functioning at peak performance, to support him—the equivalent of your back-of-house staff. The most visual example of this is the pit stop. An excellent pit stop is as beautiful and graceful as a ballet. Each person knows exactly what to do, and they must execute flawlessly. NASCAR races are measured in seconds and sometimes milliseconds. If even one person screws up in a pit stop—if a tire isn't staged in the right place, if someone fumbles while unscrewing the bolts—it can mean the difference between winning and losing. Likewise, in retail, your back-of-house operations can mean the difference between an excellent customer experience and a terrible one. Your front-of-house service relies on everything else in the store functioning perfectly—inventory management, human resources, software systems, and more.

While NASCAR drivers and pit crews make their work look almost effortless, that level of performance isn't an accident. It's a result of clearly defining each person's role, providing them the right tools and training to accomplish the job, and then *practicing*, again and again, so that they can deliver on race day.

In a store, every day is race day, so you need to practice flawless operations.

A GREAT CUSTOMER EXPERIENCE REQUIRES FLAWLESS OPERATIONS

You could do everything right—leadership, branding, service, merchandising, omnichannel, and marketing—but if your operations are not on point, the entire customer experience can be derailed. Having flawless operations means making your company run like a well-oiled machine. It's about creating repeatable processes so you can function at your best *every day*. Without excellent operations, it's so easy to fall apart. A single unexpected challenge can quickly snowball, damaging the shopping experience for multiple customers.

Operations are absolutely critical, but they're often overlooked. Especially in the cannabis industry, retailers tend to jury-rig their operations. The first year you're open is a struggle. You have so many kinks to work out. You have to figure out where to put your cash at night, who restocks the shelves, how to coordinate deliveries from multiple vendors, and on and on. Because you have so much to account for, the tendency is to figure out solutions that are "good enough" but not optimized.

The result is your operations are a bit like a wobbly, ramshackle shed. The structure will hold in most instances, but if a storm comes, the first big gust of wind can knock it all down. Somebody breaks in, and it turns out your safe wasn't secure enough. A key employee has a family emergency and can't come into work, and you discover that no one else knows the merchandising layout well enough to restock effectively. A vendor asks to make their delivery on a different day, but your interdepartment communication breaks down, and no one is there to receive the shipment.

Having flawless operations becomes increasingly important as you scale. With one store, you can easily control what happens and adapt as needed. Once you expand, you now need to create a repeatable, consistent customer experience across multiple stores, often in very different locations, with different floor plans, run by different staff. Your customers expect that every time they walk into your store, you're at peak performance. If they're a particularly loyal customer, they might let one poor experience slide, but in many cases, if you let a customer slip through the cracks even one time, you'll lose them for good. So every day, you have to be perfect.

A *ton* is included under the umbrella of operations. I've actually already touched briefly on operations in previous chapters. For instance, thoughtfully designing your pickup and delivery processes is a part of operations, as is planning ahead for how you will do inventory audits. I could easily write an entire book on operations alone, but for simplicity's sake, in this chapter I will focus on what I see as the key aspects of operations that will become exponentially more important as you scale. I will cover both processes (the step-by-step actions your employees take to complete a given task) and systems (the technological tools, both software and hardware, that you use to keep your store running smoothly). Let's get started.

ASSESS YOUR
CURRENT OPERATIONS

Improving your operations begins with understanding your baseline. If you've been operating for any amount of time, you've likely already established certain procedures. You might perceive your processes as being fantastic, but you should take the time to analyze them to ensure they're as effective as they can be.

The effectiveness of your operations can be difficult, but not impossible to measure and track. A good place to start is your customer surveys and reviews. If your operations are lacking in any one area, you'll often find similar customer complaints. Maybe customers regularly complain about long lines, out-of-stock products, or missing products in delivery orders. If a problem happens one time, you can probably chalk it up to a fluke, but once it becomes a pattern, you need to assess your operations. Somewhere, a process or system may have broken down, and you need to get to the root of the problem to truly fix it. Perhaps lines are long because your point-of-sale (POS) system is clunky and slow. Maybe you keep losing track of inventory because you haven't properly trained employees on how to barcode items. Perhaps every time a delivery order is missing products it's because the order was large enough to be broken into two bags, and you don't have a clear process for making sure those bags stay together.

In addition to looking at customer surveys and reviews, talk to your staff. Ask them about pain points in their work. Is there anything they do on a regular basis that is unnecessarily difficult or complicated? That's a hint your operations could be better optimized. Also ask them for suggestions to improve your processes, especially as related to things that have fallen or could fall through the cracks. Your staff are the ones actually carrying out your operations day in and day out. If something isn't working, they likely know it.

Finally, you can look at overall store metrics, like daily sales, top-selling items, employee turnover, on-time deliveries, and so on. Anytime a key metric is significantly worse than what you expected, you should take a look at your operations. If your number one top-selling item suddenly becomes unpopular, it's worth a closer look. Maybe something went wrong in restocking, and it never made it back out onto the shelves. If your deliveries are taking 30 percent longer than they used to, maybe you need to hire another driver. If turnover has jumped, perhaps your hiring or onboarding process needs to be refined.

We tend to be creatures of habit, so make sure the habits of your store are good ones. Don't let the excuse "We've always done it this way" justify poor operations.

ESTABLISH STANDARD OPERATING PROCEDURES: DOCUMENT, DOCUMENT, DOCUMENT!

As you assess and refine your operations, you want to establish standard operating procedures (SOPs). SOPs are step-by-step written instructions for how to accomplish the various tasks of your store. A lack of proper SOP documentation is one of the most common mistakes cannabis retailers make.

Say you have a great store manager, Jill, who was previously the manager at a clothing boutique. Because of her retail background, she was able to establish a lot of great processes at your store—how to open and close the register, how to handle customers dissatisfied with their products, how to mark down sale items, how to train staff, and more. Everything in your store is operating flawlessly. Then Jill's mother gets sick, and she needs to move out of state. All of a sudden, you realize that Jill was the glue holding your store together. Now that she's gone, all the knowledge she carried in her head—the dozens of things she did to ensure an excellent customer experience—are gone too.

To avoid finding yourself in that situation, you need written documentation of your processes: SOPs. That way, your operations do not rely on a single employee's presence. If an employee calls out sick or leaves the company entirely, you will still know exactly what to do. Written documentation also provides a standard for you to use across your company, letting you replicate a consistent customer experience at all your stores.

Written documentation is particularly useful when you need to make a change in a process. Let's say you have to change banks, and now, when cashing out the drawers at the end of the day, the person who is closing needs to include different information on the deposit slip. It's a relatively simple change, but if you have three stores, each with five different individuals who take turns closing, it gets more complicated. If you don't write it down, I promise you it won't be done properly.

So document *everything*. The script for your greeter. The onboarding process. How to fulfill pickup orders. How to apply discounts at the register. Pay attention to daily and weekly processes as well as more irregular processes. You're likely have a very specific, clear SOP for opening and closing your store, because you do it every day. Do you also have SOPs for what to do when inventory is about to expire, when a customer is upset, and when you want to launch a new product? Without SOPs, your staff will end up reinventing the wheel every time these situations arise, leading to inconsistencies and a greater chance for mistakes.

Documenting your processes will take time and effort, but it will pay off in the long run in terms of consistency and accuracy.

UPGRADE YOUR TRAINING

The foundation of good operations is good SOPs, but ultimately, the success of your operations comes down to people. It's your people who will execute the SOPs, and you need them to execute flawlessly. You ensure this through practice and training. You should employ two basic types of training: onboarding (the training a new employee receives to introduce them to the company and teach them how to perform their role) and continuing development (all the training that comes after onboarding). All your employees need training, but I will use sales associates as my example since they are the ones interacting most directly with customers.

Cannabis retail is unique in that your sales associates will need not only basic retail training (how to run the cash register, how to interact with customers, how to clean the store, etc.) but also extensive cannabis education. Early on, the easiest and most cost effective solution for onboarding may be to purchase third-party training. You can find budtender training programs and certifications to teach your sales associates the basics. As long as the training is aligned with your store brand and goals, it's a perfectly fine solution.

Eventually, though, you will want to develop your own proprietary training. Having your own training will allow you to get specific and go beyond the basics, and you can personalize everything to your brand and customer experience. Plus, as you grow and do onboarding more frequently, it can be more cost effective to have your own training. In developing your own training, think about what you need to teach new employees, in what order you will teach the material, and how you will teach it. Because everybody learns differently, you should try to incorporate a number of teaching styles. For example, if all your training material is text-based, you're not being fair to someone who is a visual learner. Ideally, you will use a mix of written material, videos, one-on-one discussions, and hands-on learning.

Remember that you don't want any key information to be stored only in someone's head. Be sure to document *everything* to do with your training. For instance, maybe part of your current onboarding process includes having new employees shadow a veteran sales associate. You should have clear written guidelines for what tasks the veteran sales associate needs to show the new employees. How to make recommendations based on terpene profiles? How to process returns? How to make novice users feel comfortable? Without clear guidelines and goals, something could easily be overlooked and missed in the training. Your documentation should be clear enough that if your normal trainer is out on vacation for two weeks, someone else can step in and take over.

In case you're currently freaking out, *you don't need to do this all at once.* Your training library is something you will build over time. Start by simply creating an outline for your onboarding. List everything that needs to be covered, in chronological order. Then focus on adding one new resource to your training manual at a time.

For continuing development, the best thing you can do is be consistent. Continuing development often happens more informally, in coaching sessions, and one of the biggest challenges is feeling like a broken record. It's tempting to think, *I've already told them this before, so I don't need to tell them again.* Your sales associates have to remember a surprising amount of information. They are bound to forget things here and there, so reminders are always welcome. In addition to one-on-one coaching, you can periodically do mini training sessions with all your sales associates. This could be as easy as giving them a verbal reminder of standard operating procedure during your standup meeting, doing a role-play exercise, or printing an article for everyone to read and discuss.

While it's most critical to train your sales associates, remember that everyone must perform their jobs well in order to provide a good customer experience. These same principles of training should be applied to all your roles.

STREAMLINE COMMUNICATION

As you scale and your staff gets bigger, communication becomes more and more important. If you're planning to have a chain of stores over the long term, you can expect to have a number of departments:

- Store operations (your existing store team, including the store manager, sales associates, onsite inventory control staff, delivery drivers, etc.)
- Merchandising
- Website management
- Marketing
- Inventory management
- Human resources
- Finance
- Security and loss prevention

For your operations to run smoothly, all these different departments need to work together. As an example, let's look at what it takes to effectively roll out a new product. The merchant needs to find and pick the product and cut a deal with the vendor. Inventory management then needs to place the order. Finance must ensure the order is paid. The store manager has to tell sales associates about the new product and make sure it is displayed properly in the store, according to whatever map the merchandising department has created. The website manager has to update the website and online ordering system with the new product information. If you decide to run a promotion for the new product, marketing has to coordinate with store operations to implement the sale. If the new product is a high-ticket item that could be easily shoplifted, security and loss prevention need to be looped in so they can prepare. Meanwhile, HR is helping to hire employees and ensure they're content, so that all these departments can function properly.

Gets complicated pretty quickly, right? Now multiply all of that across several stores, and you are going to need some *stellar* communication processes and systems.

With small teams, the most effective way to communicate with your store is for each person to simply pick up the phone and call the store manager. As you get bigger, you need to streamline the communication process and create clear guidelines for how information is cascaded through the company. If you have five stores and no streamlined communication process, then that means each time a department needs to communicate something to the stores, they have to make five calls. Simultaneously, each store manager is bombarded with information. In a single day, they could receive a call from the inventory planner, merchant, marketing team, and finance, each with a request. Imagine having four different bosses all asking different things of you! That's too many bosses, and it puts the store manager in the challenging position of figuring out what to prioritize and how to coordinate different, potentially conflicting requests. With so many lines of communication shooting back and forth and crisscrossing in the company, it's not a question of if, but when miscommunication will occur.

The way traditional retailers manage their communication is to have a communication/training department at the corporate headquarters level. Each store is essentially placed in a bubble. Instead of the merchant or inventory planner contacting the store directly, they contact the communication/training department, which then consolidates and distributes the information to every store. This way, you know that every store gets the same information, and each store has a single point of contact.

The purpose of the communication/training department is to make sure every store is on the same page, so in addition to communicating changes and new information, they are also responsible for the maintenance of the standard operating procedures, aka the training manual. If you have multiple stores, you want them to all have the same SOPs. Not only will this ensure a more consistent customer experience, but it will save time and energy. There's no point in re-creating documentation for the same task multiple times. It's far more efficient to have a central communication/training department in charge of all your training materials and SOPs.

Even for a large national retailer like Office Depot, the communication/training department tends to be small—perhaps six people total. For most cannabis retailers, just two people could run this department fairly effectively, with one person focused on communication and the other on training.

Considering the department will be small, it's important to have a good communication system in place. Rather than having your communication manager play phone tag with everyone in the company, create a communication portal. Your communication portal is where all training material and SOPs can be stored. It can also include metrics, task lists, and newsletters. Think of it as your company bible—the single resource containing all the knowledge about your company. At Office Depot, our communication portal was essentially a restricted access website. Only the communication/training department could update the website, and each user had personal login information, so they could control who in the company saw what. The store manager saw certain information, the merchant saw something else, and so on.

For your stores to operate flawlessly, you must be able to communicate clearly and consistently with each one, which means you need communication processes and a communication system.

KEEP TRACK OF AND MANAGE
YOUR INVENTORY

As you grow, the amount of inventory you must handle will grow as well. At the start, you may have just one person in charge of managing inventory.

With time, this can easily expand to an entire department, and once you have multiple stores, your inventory function will break down into two areas: inventory management (a corporate headquarters function) and inventory control (an individual store function).

Plan Ahead with Inventory Management

Inventory management is all about forecasting and planning, ensuring you have the right products at the right time. There are two golden rules in inventory management:

1. Don't run out of products, especially popular, top-selling items.
2. Don't let products expire.

Excellent operations in inventory management means having clear processes and rules to determine how much product to purchase and when to order more, as well as an alert system to identify soon-to-expire or obsolete items and a process for how to offload excess inventory (typically through promotions). To better optimize your reordering process, prevent out-of-stocks, and identify items that may expire or have become obsolete, you can use *days of supply*.

Let's say you sell an average of ten White Widow pre-rolls each day, and you have one hundred White Widow pre-rolls in stock. Total stock (one hundred) divided by average inventory sold in a day (ten) gets you your days of supply—ten, in this case. If it takes five days for your vendor to fulfill an order, then you want to make sure you place an order *before* you hit five days of supply left. You always want to give yourself a little wiggle room. Days of supply is based on the average amount you sell each day, and you could easily sell more than average, especially on a weekend or a holiday. Then you could find yourself out of stock on a popular item and potentially losing sales.

Days of supply can also alert you to when action needs to be taken on soon-to-expire or obsolete items. If you have a product that is going to expire in fourteen days, and you have sixty days of supply, then clearly you need to do something to move that product more quickly, before it expires. A go-to strategy is to put it on sale. Once it expires, you won't be able to sell it, so it's better to get whatever money you can for it than have to throw it away.

A very high days-of-supply number can also be an indication that a product is entering obsolescence, especially if that number has been getting higher and higher even though you haven't ordered any more product. Maybe you simply need to move the item to a better spot in the store or make sure sales associates are recommending it when appropriate, but if those strategies don't work, it's time to dump whatever stock you have and remove the item from your inventory.

Having a team to regularly monitor your inventory levels, forecast your sales at a product and category level, and plan shipments accordingly will be critical to optimizing your profitability and ensuring you're operating efficiently.

Stay Organized with Inventory Control

Inventory control is how inventory is managed on the store level. You need to be able to account for every item in your store, knowing exactly *what* you have and *where* you have it. Proper inventory control is critical to remain compliant with state laws and reporting guidelines, and it helps with theft reduction measures. If you don't know exactly how much product you have and where, how will you know if any goes missing? Inventory control is also key to a smooth customer experience, ensuring you are able to quickly and efficiently fill customer orders.

The biggest operational challenge of inventory control in the cannabis industry is *barcodes*. In traditional retail, barcodes are standardized. You can pick up a box of Kraft macaroni and cheese at any grocery store, whether it's Kroger, Publix, or Target, and the cashier will be able to scan the barcode and have the price pop up in their system. In the cannabis industry, though, there is an absence of standardized barcoding. If you have products without barcodes, it is *incredibly* difficult to keep track of them. Step one of improving your inventory operations is thus ensuring that every product has a barcode. To accomplish that, you may need to print your own store barcodes and hand-label each item. Obviously, this can be very time-consuming, especially as you scale, so the ideal solution is to work with your suppliers and insist they use a full barcode structure.

Once everything has a barcode, you can electronically track it using inventory management software and handheld barcode scanning devices. As soon as a shipment comes into your store, you need a process for how those items are added into your inventory system. You then need to think about how you will store the items so you can easily find them when needed. The more inventory you have, the more organized you need to be.

Say you stock fifty different types of vape cartridges and have one thousand units of each. In the middle of a busy Saturday, you run out of Blue Dream cartridges on the floor. First of all, you need a clear process for how you will ensure products are replenished when needed. If customers, and sometimes sales associates, see an empty spot, they may mistakenly assume that product is out of stock when you actually have more in the back. Maybe you have sales associates do periodic walk-throughs of the store to check for items that are running low. If all your products are locked up and require a sales associate to pull them from the case, then perhaps you have your sales associates replenish anytime they sell the last of an item. Maybe you never want your sales associates to leave the floor, and you instead have them radio a back-room employee to bring out additional stock when needed.

Whatever the process, when you need more Blue Dream cartridges, your employees need to be able to find them easily and quickly. You might have multiple storage rooms with dozens of shelves and hundreds of bins, so this is no small task. A good system is to label your shelves numerically and your bins alphabetically (or vice versa). When you input inventory into your system, include the exact location—like storage room 1, shelf 5, bin A. Then, employees can easily look up any SKU (barcode) in the store and find not only how many units you have of that item but their exact location.

With clear processes in place so that you always know exactly what you have in stock and where it is (inventory control)—as well as clear processes to ensure you have the right inventory when you need it (inventory management)—you'll be able to create a more consistently delightful experience for your customers.

INVEST IN HUMAN RESOURCES

An excellent customer experience cannot be achieved without fantastic teams, and human resources is critical in selecting and supporting your team. As your company and staff grow, you will benefit from investing in HR, whether you build your own in-house HR department or hire a third-party HR company or consultant.

The first big responsibility of HR is assisting in hiring. Some companies treat hiring willy-nilly, with an attitude that any warm body can do the job, but if you're not carefully vetting people for a given role, you are introducing risk to your customer experience. Remember that many of our customers have a lot of emotions tied up in cannabis. We can't afford to have staff that are good; we need them to be *great*. Your staff will make or break you, and HR can help you standardize and improve your recruiting practices to ensure you're hiring the best people possible. They can work with you to identify the traits needed for each role. For example, for your front-of-house staff, you're probably looking for somebody who is friendly and outgoing and can relate to people, while for back-of-house staff, you'll likely want somebody with a high attention to detail who is good with numbers and is comfortable being in front of a computer all day. HR can also create an interview guide, with the types of questions to ask and what you should be looking for in candidates' answers.

One of the most valuable things HR does, in my opinion, is screening and filtering applicants. A *lot* of people want to work in the cannabis industry. The last time I posted a cannabis position online, I was flooded with responses—literally hundreds. Some people internet-stalked me, found my phone number, and called me directly. The number of responses and the effort people put into applying was partly flattering but mostly overwhelming. I will never post a job again, because I simply do not have the time or energy to field all the responses. Instead, I've chosen to hire an HR recruiter to find me applicants. Instead of having to sort through hundreds of responses, I pick from a much smaller, high-quality pool.

In addition to helping with hiring, HR performs a whole host of duties, from handling administrative necessities to making employees feel taken care of. They can manage employee benefits, like health insurance and 401(k)s, and help write your employee handbook, laying out the company's policies against sexual harassment, workplace violence, and so on. They can also establish diversity, equity, and inclusion practices, which are especially important in our industry due to the racial injustices that have been wrapped up in cannabis. Tax forms, payroll processing, direct deposit setup, disciplinary action—it all falls under HR.

Good operations rely on your people, and HR is in charge of hiring and managing people, so one of the best investments you can make as you grow is HR.

Three Quick-and-Dirty Operations Tips

1. **Get walkie-talkies for your staff.** Especially if you have a larger store, equipping your staff with walkie-talkies can make communication far easier and eliminate roadblocks that would otherwise disrupt your operations. Say a sales associate doesn't know the answer to a customer's question or needs a restock from the back room. With the push of a button, they can get in touch with someone who can help them. Essentially, walkie-talkies allow your employees to still function as a team even when they're not in the same area.

2. **Establish processes for cleanliness.** Your customers will judge you based on the cleanliness of your store, so establish clear processes for how and when you will clean as part of your operations. Do you clean some things at close, some at open, some throughout the day? Also make sure you have a process for ensuring that the tasks are being carried out. For instance, at any major retailer, you will likely find a clipboard documenting who last inspected the bathroom and when, so management can confirm the bathroom is being cleaned regularly.

3. **Send new sales associates on a scavenger hunt.** Your staff needs practice to execute flawlessly. A great way for your sales associates to practice and familiarize themselves with your product selection and store layout is to send them on a scavenger hunt. Give them a list of products and have them go through the store to find them.

CHOOSE YOUR SYSTEMS CAREFULLY

For any store to run smoothly, you need not just good processes and talented people, but excellent systems. As you scale and serve more customers, effective, easy-to-use technological tools become invaluable. Good systems will help you to accomplish tasks more quickly, reduce mistakes, and stay owrganized across multiple stores.

In selecting the systems for your store, keep these three tips in mind:

1. **Look for cannabis-specific technological solutions.** Unfortunately, many traditional software solutions will not work for cannabis companies. This is yet another area where we face additional challenges due to the stigma of cannabis and its Schedule I status. In particular, payroll software can be a pain to find because of the banking restrictions we operate under. Fortunately, some companies have recognized this gap in the market and offer cannabis-specific solutions. By looking for cannabis-specific tools, not only do you know they'll work, but they often have helpful features specific to our industry, like point-of-sale (POS) systems that come with a built-in ID scanner and age verification.

2. **Prioritize integration.** Remember the earlier example about how your different departments must work together? The same is true for your systems. Anytime your systems need to use the same information but can't talk to each other, you're increasing your workload by having to input the same information in multiple places. Plus, a lack of integration can lead to mistakes that harm the customer experience. If your inventory, POS, and e-commerce systems don't all connect, for example, then you'll have a very difficult time maintaining accurate inventory numbers. You could sell out of an item in-store, but then your online store isn't updated, and somebody places an order for that item. Now you're going to have an unhappy customer.

3. **Get demos.** You can read all about systems, but to really figure out whether a piece of software or hardware will work for your store, you need to see it in action. Most companies offer demos, and some will even personalize the demo for you, showcasing how their software can meet your specific needs.

The needs of each store (or chain of stores) will be slightly different, but these eight systems are fairly common:

1. Point-of-sale (POS)
2. Inventory
3. HR
4. E-commerce
5. Customer Relationship Management (CRM)
6. Accounting

7. Analytics

8. Planogramming

You may already have systems in place for some of these, but don't assume your current system is the best option. Just as our industry is an explosion of innovation when it comes to cultivation and manufacturing, the systems available to us have been rapidly evolving. A year ago, I would've recommended Cova to most cannabis retailers for their POS. Right now, I'm impressed with Flowhub. In another year or two, who knows what incredible new solutions will be available to us. Any specific recommendations I give could quickly become outdated, so instead, here's a general breakdown of what you should be looking for in each system.

Point-of-Sale (POS)

From a technology perspective, the hub of the customer experience is the POS system, so you need it to be fast, reliable, and easy to use. You likely already have a POS system. It's one of the few systems you *have* to have to open. You're also probably not shopping for a new POS system right now because switching can be a monumental task. However, there are two situations in which it is worth making the switch, despite the work involved:

1. **Your POS system does not integrate well with other systems.** Since your POS is the hub of the customer experience, it's absolutely critical that it connects to your other primary systems. Your POS should include or be able to integrate with inventory, e-commerce, CRM (particularly the loyalty program), accounting, analytics, and planogramming software. Even if you do not currently use one of these other systems, you should expect that

you will use it at some point in the future. Switching your POS system will only get more difficult as you grow, so prepare for integration now.

2. **You (or your staff) really dislike your current POS system.**
The other good reason to switch is if you or your staff are dissatisfied with your current POS system. I'm not talking about mild annoyances but legitimate complaints that are disrupting your workflow. Maybe the system is not at all intuitive, and it takes ages to train new employees on it. Perhaps you run regular promotions, but your POS system won't let you set up automatic discounts. Maybe it won't let you customize the data fields for your SKUs so you can add your own product descriptions. If your current POS system is creating problems for you, they'll only get worse.

Your POS is the heart of your systems, so it needs to meet all your current needs and also be robust enough to meet your future needs as you grow.

Inventory

Ideally, a good inventory system will include both inventory control features, allowing you to manage your inventory inside the store and do audits, as well as inventory management features, giving you robust planning capabilities.

After integration (particularly with your POS and e-commerce systems and ideally your analytics software too), your inventory system should do these three things:

1. **Connect with mobile hardware.** You really need handheld, mobile inventory devices in your store. Mobile hardware allows your staff to easily scan a barcode and check the inventory from

anywhere in the store. They also let you do audits far more easily. At the beginning, you might be able to get away with counting inventory by hand or carrying products over to your registers to scan them, but as you scale, that's going to be far too time-consuming.

2. **Provide multilocation functionality.** Though you might have only one location right now, you want your inventory system to be able to handle multiple locations so it can grow with you. Once you have more than one location, you need to know not just your total inventory numbers, but the inventory for each of your stores.

3. **Track expiring product and provide restock alerts.** You should have someone keeping an eye on your inventory on a regular basis, but to make their job easier and prevent anything from falling through the cracks, you want an inventory system that can alert you when you're running low on stock or have products that are about to expire.

After the POS system, an inventory system is one of the most important systems to implement early on.

HR

A good HR system allows you to organize and control the entire employee experience, from the hiring process to final termination. The better your HR system is, the more confidence your employees will have in you, as a good HR system makes your company feel more credible and professional. Here are some things your HR system should do:

- **Organize your hiring process.** Ideally, your HR system will connect to whatever hiring platform you use, like Indeed. It will let you filter your applicants, schedule interviews, and leave comments and notes about candidates. Once you decide to hire someone, you should be able to send them an offer letter right from the system.

- **Manage your paperwork and forms.** After being hired, a new employee should be able to log into the system to fill out all the necessary paperwork—tax forms, cannabis worker permits, and so on. This may not sound like a big deal, but it is a huge time saver and can help prevent things from falling through the cracks. The alternative is to have employees fill these forms out by hand and then pay someone else to input them electronically or mail them to the appropriate places. Plus, with cannabis worker permits, which must be done annually, a good HR system will let you automatically remind your employees to renew their permits so that you don't have to keep track of dozens of different renewal deadlines.

- **Manage payroll.** If your employees aren't paid on time, they're not going to be happy, which will trickle down to your customer experience. Your HR system should let you easily manage your payroll, including offering direct deposit and taking care of all taxes you must withhold. To do this effectively, your HR systems need to be integrated with your accounting system.

- **Properly administer benefits.** You should be able to manage all the benefits you offer—health insurance, 401(k)s, and so on—from one place in your HR system.

- **Manage time and attendance.** Your HR system should include a clock-in and clock-out capability to track your employees' hours. Ideally, it will also have robust scheduling capabilities, making it easy for you to create schedules and for employees to view their schedules, track their paid time off, and put in requests for time off.

These are just a sampling of the potential capabilities of HR software. So much is involved with an HR system that I recommend you consult with a professional (either in-house or third-party HR) for recommendations.

E-Commerce

I already talked in-depth about e-commerce in the omnichannel chapter, so I'll keep this short. Your e-commerce system should let you do four major things:

1. **Easily upload item pictures and descriptions.**
2. **Let customers leave product-specific reviews.**
3. **Allow for easy filtering and sorting.**
4. **Provide capabilities for both pickup and delivery.**
   (Even if you're not currently allowed to do pickup or delivery, they may become options in the future, so plan ahead.)

Put yourself in the customer's shoes when you select an e-commerce system. Go to different cannabis websites and see what it feels like to place an order with different software. Choose one that is easy and delightful to use, keeping in mind that it needs to integrate with your POS, inventory, CRM, accounting, and analytics systems.

Customer Relationship Management (CRM)

CRM software will allow you to manage how you interact with new and existing customers as well as run things like your loyalty program and automated text and emails. Your CRM software should help you gather and organize data about your customers' behavior then use it to define your marketing strategies. With this data, your system should then help you map out and manage your customer journey, on a personalized level, so you can increase customer retention and recurring purchases.

As always, you want to look for solid integration with your other systems. On top of that, here's what a solid CRM will let you do:

- **Customize your loyalty program.** Your system should give you a lot of flexibility in designing your loyalty program. Are customers going to get points for every visit or every dollar they spend? Will you ever offer double points? What kind of rewards will you have? Do you want tiered rewards, where customers can unlock more rewards the more points they earn? A good marketing system should be able to do it all.

- **Allow customers to see their loyalty rewards.** Simply having a loyalty program is a great step in customer retention, but for your loyalty program to be most effective, customers should be able to see their points accumulating. Sometimes cannabis stores will have a loyalty program, but the only time customers know how many points they have or what rewards they've earned is at checkout. So most of the time, they're not coming to the store *because* of the loyalty program; the loyalty program is an afterthought. In contrast, if customers know ahead of time that they have a reward to use— or are close to earning a reward—they might make a special trip just to rack up points or use their reward.

- **Automate your marketing emails and texts.** Imagine how time-consuming it would be to manually send out all your marketing emails and texts. You would never get anything else done! A marketing system will let you set up automatic emails and texts based on a variety of triggers—like spending milestones, birthdays, anniversaries, or a sudden drop in a customer's visitation frequency.

- **Ensure compliance with relevant laws.** Federal laws (like the Telephone Consumer Protection Act) regulate how businesses can communicate with customers. Especially with text messages, you need to be careful you're not breaking any rules. A good marketing system will have built-in features to address this (like a "double opt-in" procedure to ensure customers have consented to receiving messages).

With so much competition in the cannabis space, your marketing is critical. A good system will help you be much more personalized and thoughtful in your marketing.

Accounting

I'm not an accountant, so I'll keep this one short and sweet too. You have to pay your taxes, or your company will go broke. Taxes are complicated, particularly in the cannabis industry and especially if you operate in more than one state. I highly recommend hiring a certified public accountant (CPA) who has experience in the cannabis industry and, as you scale, a CFO. Let them guide your decision for accounting software. QuickBooks is fairly standard and usually integrates well with other systems.

Analytics

Data analytics is absolutely critical to store operations. It's how you maximize your current efficiency as well as prepare for future trends. Nowadays, thanks to technology, we have access to more—and more detailed—data than ever. While all this data is a good thing, you really need a solid system to be able to collect, organize, and assess it properly.

Aside from integration with your other systems, here's what else a good analytics system should do:

- **Track everything you care about.** Basket size and mix, revenue, top sellers, promotions effectiveness—whatever you care about, you should be able to customize your analytics system to track it. Look for systems that are flexible, as what you want to track today may be different from what you want to track a year from now.
- **Make the data comprehensible.** A good analytics system doesn't just provide data; it presents the data in a way that is useful for you. If all you wanted was a giant list of numbers, you could pull it from one of your other systems. Your analytics system should have data visualization, with graphs and tables, so you can clearly see what the data is telling you.
- **Allow you to export the data.** I've found that sometimes, even with a good analytics system, I want to export the data to Microsoft Excel to do additional analysis.
- **Provide big-picture data beyond your store.** The best analytics systems will anonymize and compile data from all their users to determine statewide and/or nationwide trends. This is *huge*. While your store-specific data is very valuable, it's restricted to your current customers. Broader industry data gives you information about cannabis consumers as a whole—aka, all your *potential* customers. This data provides important context, letting you understand common price points, trends in buying behavior, and more. Note that analytics systems with national data often have a higher price

tag. If you have stores across many states, the cost might be worth it, but if you operate in a single state, I recommend just looking for statewide data.

- **Protect your data.** Especially when working with customer information, you need to keep your data secure. A good analytics system will have robust security measures.

Running a store can sometimes feel like a guessing game, with endless trial and error to figure out what works for your customers. A good analytics system can take the guesswork out of your decisions, letting you grow faster and more efficiently.

Planogramming

The more locations you have, the more critical a planogramming system is. Planogramming software is also helpful if you want to test out several different merchandising strategies, like the effectiveness of various end caps or cash wrap displays. Here are some things your planogramming system should do:

- **Integrate with other systems.** At this point, you're probably sick of me harping on integration, but it really is important. If your planogramming software can't connect to your POS or inventory systems, you'll have to input every single product you sell! You'll also have to manually update it every time you get a new product or stop selling something. If you can connect your planogramming system to your POS and analytics systems, you can get helpful information about which sections of the store sell the best (and worst) and the effects of different merchandising layouts.

- **Allow macro and micro planning.** You want to be able to plan out your overall macro store layout (e.g., edibles in this case, pre-rolls in that case, etc.) as well as your micro layouts (the specific products that appear in each individual case).
- **Be easy to use.** Many planogram systems will have a drag-and-drop interface, which makes them easy to use.
- **Provide scale modeling.** For your planogram to be most helpful, it will be a scale model of your store. Your planogramming system should have the option of including product dimensions so you can plan out displays on a fine-tuned level. Note that this means you will need to collect these dimensions from suppliers as part of the product's digital assets.

A good planogramming system will help you maximize the effectiveness of your merchandising and keep your store layouts consistent across multiple stores, so while it may not be an immediate priority, it's good to keep in mind.

We live in a technological world, so good systems aren't simply an advantage but a necessity to compete. These eight systems are just a foundation. You may decide to implement other systems not listed here. The goal is to make your employees' jobs as easy as possible so they can focus on flawless execution and service.

GET HELP, IMPROVE, GROW, REPEAT

The moment you relax and think you're done improving your operations, you've lost—game over. Especially since accidental success is so common in the cannabis industry, it's easy to have poor operations without even realizing it. Eventually, though, you'll be outpaced by the retailers who execute flawless operations. Make it a practice to constantly review and upgrade your operations so you can be the one outpacing the competition.

If you're feeling overwhelmed, take a deep breath. Here's the key: while you'll eventually need to do everything in this book, you aren't meant to do it all at once. You always have to function under the constraints of time, money, and resources. Instead of struggling to figure out how to do everything, focus on figuring out what to do *next*. At least once every year, take the time to do a strategic assessment: What have you already accomplished? What still needs to be done? Which of those things are the highest priority, and why? This is something I do all the time—not only for the companies I consult with, but for my own business as well.

Here's the second key: *you're not meant to do this alone.* Major retailers have entire departments dedicated to each of the topics I've covered: leadership, branding, service, merchandising, omnichannel, marketing, operations. As you grow, you can begin building out your staff, and if you're not ready to support a full-time position, you can always hire consultants. Hiring third-party consultants is actually common practice for traditional retailers. Sometimes you're so close to your business that it's difficult for you to assess it strategically. There's tremendous value in getting another set of eyes and a different perspective on your business to determine how to best prioritize your efforts to get the most return on investment. This is exactly what I do for many of the retailers I work with. Sometimes all you need is a little guidance to get on the right track.

There's no shame or weakness in getting help. Being a business owner is difficult under normal circumstances. Being a cannabis business owner takes things to a whole new level of challenging. When you get help, you can improve more quickly and grow your business. Then you can repeat the cycle all over again: get help, improve, grow; get help, improve, grow. That's a recipe for long-term success.

Conclusion

On December 6, 2020, I woke up early. It was my partner's birthday, and I was planning a surprise video call with family and friends for him. When I checked my phone, I found multiple missed calls, texts, and voicemails from the night before. My heart sank immediately. My brother Joe's girlfriend had left me a message: "Char, please call me."

I always knew I would get this call—technically calls, plural—one day. Every time one of my friends lost a family member to an overdose, I cried for their pain, and wondered when my own call would come. I didn't know what had happened yet, but I thought, *This is my day.*

When I called my brother's girlfriend back, it was around 6:20 in the morning. I was hit with déjà vu and had a horrible flashback of the 6:20 phone call from my grandmother telling me my father had died.

"Char, I can't do it anymore," Ayron, Joe's girlfriend, told me. "He tried to commit suicide last night. He's at a hospital somewhere. I don't know where."

My mom had just buried her dad and sister, and I couldn't bring myself to call her and tell her she might have to bury her son too. I started calling hospitals, desperate to find Joe and terrified of what I would discover when I did. When I found him, the hospital initially wouldn't give me any information. By nine o'clock, I begged, "Can you just tell me: is he alive?"

In the past couple of years, Joe had begun taking Suboxone. Suboxone is the doctor-recommended way to get off opioids: an opioid substitute that takes away physical withdrawal symptoms. It cost him thirteen dollars a day, and he had to take it every day, so it cost about $400 a month, or just under $5,000 a year. Because it was so expensive, his whole goal in life was to get off the Suboxone. Suboxone is still an opioid, so when he began weaning himself off of it, he experienced withdrawal symptoms. To deal with the withdrawal, he picked up drinking, twenty-four hours a day, seven days a week. He could get a fifth of alcohol for around seven dollars, so by replacing one addiction with another, he cut the financial burden in half.

The emotional burden, however, grew. His whole life was built around the lie of pretending to be sober. When he had a buzz, he was mean, and he pushed people away, further isolating himself. His self-confidence deteriorated. *I'm trash*, he thought. *I am a bad person. I am worthless. I mean nothing to no one.* It's really difficult to love somebody who has that much self-hate in his heart. You simply can't trust anything they say or do. He was like a porcupine—prickly on the outside but soft underneath. Every time I came near him, I didn't know if he would give me a hug or stab me in the heart.

As much pain as he caused me when he lashed out, nothing hurt as much as the thought of him being gone. The person I spoke to at the hospital must have heard that pain in my voice, because when I begged to know whether he was alive, she told me. He was in critical care, but yes, he was alive. I can't even describe the relief I felt. He still had a chance. He still had a future. At that moment, halfway across the country, I made a decision—a promise to my brother: "I'm sick of your fight with this horrid addiction, and I'm so sorry that the world exposed you to this drug. But I'm going to try to save you. You deserve to be saved." Joe didn't think he deserved to be saved. I did, though. I knew it would be scary and painful, but I was going to put myself and my family at risk, and I was going to try. He may have given up, but I was going to fight for him.

He spent two weeks in a medical detox. On Friday, December 18, my daughter's birthday, I found out he was getting discharged that Sunday. My big fear was that he would be discharged and have nowhere to go. Though his girlfriend loved him, she had reached a breaking point, and my mother wasn't in a place to take him in either. So it fell to me.

I flew from Florida to North Carolina, rented a car, and drove straight to the facility. When they released Joe, he emerged barefoot in a hospital gown. Because of COVID-19, they wouldn't even let him get dressed inside. We got food, got him dressed, and picked up some stuff from his girlfriend's house. We were supposed to spend the night and fly out the next day, but when we got to the hotel, I couldn't stand the thought of waiting there for twenty-four hours. "I don't want to sit in this hotel. I want to go home," I said, and he said, "I do too." I drove him home that night, making the whole trip in twenty hours. I'm so glad we made that decision. We weren't able to talk when he was in detox, but we talked for hours on the car ride. We cried. We laughed so hard it hurt. We talked about his future.

For the first time in his life since that first OxyContin at fourteen years old, Joe was physically off all drugs. Addiction never fully goes away, but he was in recovery. He had support and love, and he had *hope*. I had my brother back, and it was wonderful. We spent Christmas together as a family—my partner and daughter, my mom, and both my brothers. We watched scary movies. We reminisced. It was such a blessing having him around. He made the best tzatziki, pork souvlaki, and Greek salad, and with me being so busy, he was the one who made sure everyone was fed. He did the dishes too and helped out with lawn work. The best part was just hearing his laughter in the house.

While I worked at my desk, he would sit behind me working on his résumé and applying for jobs. He'd hear me talk about cannabis, and he was so curious. No one had ever told him that cannabis was safe. Joe and I didn't think it was a good idea for him to use any drugs at this point in his life, so he didn't use cannabis, but we'd say to each other, "If only John had cannabis!" or "Fuck Richard Sackler!" We would laugh, but it hurt at the same time, because of the truth buried there. If Purdue Pharma hadn't pushed opioids on our country or if John had access to cannabis, my brother's life would have been completely different. He had so much shame related to being a drug addict, and learning about the societal circumstances that had contributed to his addiction helped. He still had to be accountable and make his own decisions. He had a beast inside of him, and every day, he had to wake up and face it. Knowing about the Big Lies didn't take the beast away, but it made his fight a little easier.

In March 2021, I went on spring break with my daughter and a friend. The day I left, after three months of being clean, Joe took some Percocet. I don't know where he got them or how, but it sent him into a spiral. While I was gone, he had a small relapse with alcohol. I have a Ring camera, so I literally watched him do it. It was very emotional for me. I confronted him about it. "You have to stop," I told him. "You have to. This is your second chance, brother. We just got you clean, and you've been so good. Don't get addicted again." He kept drinking, though. I couldn't have that happening in my house, and I couldn't let myself be an enabler, so that Friday, I had to ask him to leave. When I talked to him, he still had a buzz, and he lashed out at me. He ended up sleeping outside that night, which absolutely killed me.

On Saturday, he woke up with determination. He went to a church that had an organization called Changing Lives. While at the church, he had a seizure in their bathroom. They called 911, and he went to the hospital. He was released a few hours later, and he went back to the church for an AA meeting. I talked to him that evening, and he told me, "Char, I don't want to be like this. I'm going to get help." He told me about the calls he'd already made to find himself a treatment facility. He was so proud of himself, and I was proud of him too.

I booked a hotel room for him for two nights. Once he got there, I called him again. He was sad he'd relapsed, but he had hope in his voice. He was doing the right thing, and he wasn't doing it for me, but for himself. I encouraged him, wanting him to believe that he could fight the beast. I broke down in tears and told him I loved him. He teared up and said he loved me too. My daughter got on the phone so she could tell him "I love you" as well, and we said our goodbyes. About twenty minutes later, I sent him a text saying, "Use your time wisely, brother."

The next day my spring break ended. It was a hectic day. We had to pack up and check out of the hotel, drop my friend off at the airport, and then I had to take my daughter to her play rehearsal. In the middle of all this, my mother wanted to send some food to Joe, but he wasn't responding to her texts. Then I realized that he hadn't responded to my text from the previous night, which was weird, because he always responded. I tried calling him, but he didn't pick up. At that moment, I knew, but I didn't want to say it out loud. I was still in the car with my daughter, and I didn't want to overreact.

My mom called the hotel to do a wellness check, and they said, "Ma'am, there's a situation." My mom went to the hotel, and when she pulled around the corner, there were all these police cars there. She called to tell me the news. Joe was dead. I screamed when she told me. I'd already gotten my call in December, and we were given another chance. I wasn't supposed to get a second call. This wasn't supposed to be the end of Joe's story. He was getting better. He'd had a slip, but that happens to everybody, and he was doing all the right things now. There were no drugs or alcohol in the room, and his résumé was lying out on the bed. He had two interviews lined up over the next couple of weeks.

The toxicology report revealed the cause of death to be diazepam with fentanyl—a fake Valium. I know it's easy to judge, to say he shouldn't have taken that pill, but Valium is virtually harmless. My dog has been prescribed Valium before. Joe had had a very bad day, and I'm sure he just wanted something to help him relax. He probably thought he was doing the right thing by not taking a harder drug. It shouldn't have been a death sentence, but it was.

On September 27, 2021, the DEA launched the "One Pill Can Kill" campaign to raise public awareness about counterfeit pharmaceuticals in the black market. According to the website, "The number of DEA-seized counterfeit pills with fentanyl has jumped nearly 430 percent since 2019. DEA lab testing reveals that two out of every five pills with fentanyl contain a potentially lethal dose."[86] This warning is long overdue. This issue is impacting not just addicts, but high school and college-aged kids purchasing pills through Snapchat.[87] This new trend further exacerbates the Opioid Endemic and is yet another reason that cannabis usage should be normalized and readily accessible to users over the age of twenty-one.

The day my brother died, a monarch butterfly fell in my pool. My heart and soul were broken, and seeing that butterfly struggling, about to drown, was more than I could take. *Please don't be too late*, I thought as I scooped

---

[86] DEA, "One Pill Can Kill," accessed October 27, 2021, https://www.dea.gov/onepill.

[87] Olivia Solon, "When One Pill Kills," NBC News, October 1, 2021, https://www.nbcnews.com/specials/pills-bought-on-snapchat-deadly/.

him out of the pool. He crawled from my hand up to my shoulder, then to the top of my head, and he just wouldn't leave. He stayed there for twenty minutes, drying his wings so he could fly away. I have a large patch of milkweed in my yard, and over the years, my family has raised hundreds of monarch butterflies. In all that time, I've never had a butterfly stay with me like that. In its own magical symbolism, that butterfly was my brother, and he was saying, "Char, you saved me." When the butterfly finally spread his wings and flew away, it was like my brother telling me that he was free now. His pain was gone, and he was headed to the next phase of his life.

Breaking free of addiction is a lot like a caterpillar transitioning into a butterfly. It's a difficult transformation. You're broken down and rebuilt, and you have to fight your way out of the chrysalis. Had my brother died when I received that first phone call in December, he would have died with despair in his heart, in the grips of his addiction, still a caterpillar. The only way I can cope with his loss is to believe that he stole three months from fate. In those three months, he found love and peace. He built his chrysalis and transformed into a butterfly.

I am so grateful to have had those three months, but I wanted more. Still now, all I want is more—more time, more laughs, more memories. Joe died a week before his thirty-fifth birthday. It was the first birthday he was ever afraid of, because he was worried it was too late for him to start over. I would tell him, "It's not too late. You're going to stay clean, get a good job, find a nice girl who's clean with you and understands, and you're going to knock her up and make me some nieces and nephews." He would chuckle at that idea, because I think for him, it was impossible to imagine that he could recover and have a normal life. That's all he wanted: a normal life.

It feels so unfair. He was the first person I told about this book because he was such a big reason why I was writing it. He thought it was so cool, and he was so proud of me. He will never get to read this book that he inspired. He will never get to fix up his truck like he wanted or learn new songs on the guitar. I feel cheated. He wasn't done living. After having twenty years of his life stolen by addiction, he'd only just gotten started living. When I think about my brother, a broken record starts in my head. *It's a lie, it's a lie, it's a lie.* The Big Lies surrounding cannabis killed my brother, and they continue to be perpetuated today.

People still think Black men are dangerous. It's why a white woman would call the cops on a Black man for the "crime" of birdwatching. It's why we have police officers pulling triggers and killing Black citizens. Yet in my grief, the voices of Black men were my sounds of comfort—my safety. In DRS's "Gangsta Lean," I heard my pain of losing someone too soon. In "I Tried," Bone Thugs-n-Harmony sing about their struggles on the street, but when I listen to it word for word, I can also hear my brother's pain of battling his addiction, of trying so hard but never being able to get rid of the beast. When I didn't know how I could possibly get up and keep living, Tupac's "Keep Ya Head Up" and Diddy's "Coming Home" were my beacons.

People still think cannabis is dangerous, and opioids are safe. Cannabis has never killed anyone, and the Opioid Endemic has killed more than five hundred thousand Americans. Yet OxyContin and fentanyl, the drug that killed my brother, remain Schedule II drugs, while cannabis is Schedule I. The people responsible for the Opioid Endemic have yet to serve a single day behind bars, while tens of thousands of people, disproportionately people of color, are currently incarcerated for cannabis offenses.

People still think addiction is the addict's fault. My brother told me all the time, "I just want to be better." A trusted source gave him medicine at fourteen years old, and it created a beast inside of him. My brother didn't choose to have that beast inside of him, but every day, he had to wake up and face it. Most days, he won. He was stronger than most people could ever know, and he did not deserve to die.

These lies are a disservice to every person in this country. They are a disservice to every Black American and minority that faces systemic racism, to every individual who has been addicted to an opioid, to every cannabis user who has been ostracized from society.

I'm baffled—and, frankly, outraged—that we're still fighting the stigma of cannabis, but here we are. We *have* to break this stigma. If you don't invest in the key retail functions I've laid out in this book, you are placing the longevity of your company at risk, but it's about more than that too. By being the best retailer you can be, you can help shift public perception of cannabis. You can break the stigma so that everyone who needs cannabis has access to it. *The veteran suffering from night terrors. The grandfather with arthritis. The blue-collar worker needing pain management. The young professional with anxiety.*

As cannabis retailers, we are in a unique and powerful position. We are building this industry. We can't change the past, but we can choose who we will be moving forward. In a way, we too are caterpillars right now, and we must decide whether or not we are willing to do the hard work of transforming into butterflies. Will we let ourselves be driven by profit and greed? Or will we commit to doing better, to creating a customer experience that breaks the stigma and building an industry that prioritizes not just profit, but people and purpose?

There is only one right answer. Let us choose well and welcome Grandma—and everyone who can benefit from this plant—into the dispensary.

Acknowledgments

When I think of the community that has built me, shaped my opinions, and contributed to my career, I'm grateful for such an exhaustive list of friends, family, and peers that I find it difficult to determine where to begin.

To the cannabis warriors who have spent their lives dedicated to the cause of bringing the plant back to our communities. Without you, there would be no reason for this book. I gratefully stand upon your shoulders.

To those whose lives have been impacted by the War on Drugs. My heart sits with all who were affected by this needless war, and I have many tears for the families shattered by the Opioid Endemic.

To David Kotler, my father in weed. I'm eternally grateful to you. Thank you for taking a chance on me and introducing me to this industry. And for that trip to Africa. Looking forward to a lifetime of industry partnerships.

To Lance Rogers. I wouldn't be here without your guidance and advice. You taught me so much about always doing the right thing for the client in all that we do and every decision that we make.

To Alysia Gordy. We have twenty-seven years of friendship and now are business partners too. I couldn't be in this crazy industry without your loyal support. Thank you.

To Daniel Wise, Geo Pattah, and Saad Pattah with Cake. Joining your team has been a blessing, and I'm proud to be on this journey with you! I am eternally grateful and beyond humbled for the tribute to my brother in Malibu. May it forever symbolize why the plant is greater than the pill.

To Travis "Sharky" Crosby and Ryan Hasler. Thank you for taking emotions and bringing them to life with art. I'm beyond grateful for the incredible tribute to my brother in Malibu.

To my mentor Kevin O'Meara. The best advice you ever gave me was "Always assume that people have good intentions." I believe this single-handedly shifted my perception on how to be a good team member and leader.

To Anna Shreeve. I am forever grateful for your guidance and example on how to navigate as a woman in a male-dominated industry.

To Betty Mitchell. Your grit, determination, wisdom, humor, and overall outlook on life are an inspiration. It is my pleasure to have met you, and I appreciate you joining me on this journey! Thank you for sharing your story with the world!

To Daniel KrKruc. Thank you for your loyalty and friendship and for encouraging my continued success in the industry. I'm lucky to have a friend and business partner like you.

To Wesley Clark and Tyson Hunter. I'm so blessed to call you not only clients and peers, but friends. Thank you for sticking with me since the beginning and supporting my journey to explore how cannabis should be done right.

To Fran and Chip Megyese and Bob and Gail Blazo. Thank you for always believing in me and nurturing me through life. You have been the rock that kept me grounded, and you've inspired me to keep putting one foot in front of the other.

To Cathy Haley, Elia Zechiel, Sara Glisson, Pat Oderkirk, Jim Augustine, and all the teachers in this world who invested time in me and others to make us better humans.

To Judge Robert Yampolsky. Thank you for gambling on the will and determination of a young woman. The gift of emancipation enabled my education, success, and hopefully influence in this world.

To Randy and Bonnie Schultz. Your training, support, and love in the days at BP humbly shaped my perspective on customer service.

To my dearest Nikki and all the other Nikkis in this world. I'm so sorry that you have to face this life without your dad. Always remember that he is forever an angel watching you. May you learn to understand what happened and find ways to cope that do not perpetuate the cycle.

To the Stevens family, in particular Aunt Sheila. Joey and Chucky are watching and with us. Thank you for allowing me to tell their story.

To Amy Broglin, my sister in grief. I hate the club that we are in. But Rachel Ann and Joe are protecting our journey. Our blessing here is not having to face it alone and being able to use our collective experience as a platform to shine light into darkness.

To Jenna Alish. I love you. I love you. I love you. Thank you for being my friend. I can still hardly believe it was you with me. Thank you for sharing a lifetime of understanding of parental and sibling addiction. My world is better with you in it.

To Miss Brandi Spaniola. I'm so proud of you. Thank you for letting me tell your story here. Keep sharing your story and uplifting others. It is because of you that I know recovery is possible.

To Ayron, Talyn, and Mika. Thank you for giving my brother the best years of his life. Bringing you guys joy was his greatest pleasure. He loved you all very much. You have a very special angel protecting you.

To Uncle Kenny and Dixie. Thank you for your eternal love and for standing with me through the good, bad, and ugly. Uncle Kenny, your wisdom and guidance have never let me down.

To Aunt Tina and Uncle Johnny. Thank you for your support and for sharing your experiences here. You made me a believer, and I hope that equal access will come soon to your state.

To Darrell. While not always perfect, I will forever treasure our partnership.

To Mom. I love you. Thank you for your relentless support.

To Brother Kenny. Thank you for being an incredible uncle, brother, and friend. It's up to us to move the family forward.

To my dearest Zepplyn. I am humbled and honored to be your mom. Thank you for helping me cope through the grief and for encouraging me to finish this book. When my confidence is down, your youthful wisdom never ceases to amaze me.

Recommended Reading

Atlas Shrugged, by Ayn Rand

The Carrot Principle: How the Best Managers Use Recognition to Engage Their People, Retain Talent, and Accelerate Performance, by Adrian Gostick and Chester Elton

Conscious Capitalism: Liberating the Heroic Spirit of Business, by John Mackey and Rajendra Sisodia

How the Mighty Fall: And Why Some Companies Never Give In, by Jim Collins

How to Win Friends and Influence People, by Dale Carnegie

Jim Moran: The Courtesy Man, by Jim Moran

The Leadership Pipeline: How to Build the Leadership Powered Company, by Ram Charan, Stephen Drotter, and James Noel

Lincoln on Leadership: Executive Strategies for Tough Times, by Donald T. Phillips

Moving Mountains: Lessons in Leadership and Logistics from the Gulf War, by Lt. General William G. Pagonis

Outliers: The Story of Success, by Malcolm Gladwell

Zero to One: Notes on Startups, or How to Build the Future, by Peter Thiel with Blake Masters

About the Author

I come from humble beginnings. That is the term I coined as a nice way of saying that my upbringing was terribly violent. I have spent my entire life not speaking about my past, and quite honestly, I have carried a tremendous amount of shame about it. With friends, peers, and colleagues, it has always been very uncomfortable for me to talk about it. My history makes me different from everyone else, and it has always been easier to try to blend in by not addressing or acknowledging the awful things about my childhood. No one likes drama or self-pity. Neither breeds success. So I locked my past away and did what I could to hide those stories from those who know me.

Yet for me, this book is about releasing shame, in all its forms. I have finally concluded that there is no reason for me to be ashamed of where I come from. In fact, while seemingly obvious, my past is what shaped who I am today, and frankly, it's a pure miracle that I have been able to overcome such obstacles. While it's still a little terrifying for me, I am ready to share my story with you.

It was actually only while in the process of writing this book that I began to fully understand the demons that have haunted me. One of my dad's old friends heard I now worked in cannabis, and he got in touch with me. "Do you know what your dad was?" he asked me. "He was a drugstore cowboy." I had to ask him to explain what that meant, because I'd never heard the term before. Apparently, my dad would rob drugstores during snowstorms for class A drugs and then resell them. His friend also told me stories of them smuggling Red Lebanese hash through Sweden. "We were gettin' kilos for twelve hundred dollars a pop," he said.

It was a huge epiphany for me. I remember there always being a lot of drugs in the house—guns and literal crates full of bullets too. I recall sitting in the driveway loading magazines with my brothers. While I knew it wasn't normal, I had never connected the dots before. I was a child and simply craved peace away from a household that was regularly under siege by violence.

Looking back now, so many things make more sense. My dad would take us on long trips across the country with detours into Mexico. If we were pulled over, he'd pretend that one of us kids had to puke. He hosted huge house parties and went on extravagant vacations. Even where we lived—a rural Michigan town with only three stop lights—has a new meaning for me now. Located on Highway 94, halfway between Chicago and Detroit, it was an ideal spot for moving drugs.

Never able to separate his work life from his extracurricular activities, my dad was extraordinarily violent and made very poor parenting decisions.

When I was eight, while he was in the middle of a fight with my mom, my dad punched me in the face. Drunk, he left with us kids, and when we cried for her, he dropped us off at the end of the road, and we had to walk home by ourselves in our pajamas and no shoes down a dirt road. Kenny was six, and Joe was four.

At thirteen, I was jumped by two seventeen-year-old girls. Afterward, my dad made fun of me. "You can't fight your way out of a paper bag," he told me. He had taught me that I should always throw the first punch and it wasn't acceptable to lose a fight. Girls were no exception to this rule.

Around that same age, my dad held me and my stepmom up with an AK-47, then tried to strangle me a few days later.

I could go on and on with stories like this. Yet somehow I was gifted with determination to break the chains. Somehow I knew that making my own money was my only chance, so I worked.

When I was fourteen, I started my first job making $4.85 an hour. I worked two to three jobs at a time to afford the basics, like food, clothing, and eyeglasses. I took any job I could. I worked at the farmers market, a fruit stand, a gas station, and the hardware store, and I did stints as a janitor, tutor, bartender, and waitress.

From fourteen to sixteen or seventeen, I was homeless. I couch-surfed, hopping from place to place to try to find a home.

At sixteen, I was legally emancipated from my parents.

At eighteen, I graduated high school. I was eleventh in my class and senior class president. I earned a full-ride scholarship and put myself through college, without a single cent from my parents.

Two months after I graduated from Michigan State University, my dad committed suicide. My brother was living with me at the time and began using heroin. I watched him withdraw on my couch.

When I was twenty-seven, my grandmother, the family matriarch and my hero and mentor, developed dementia and Alzheimer's. I took care of her for three years, while working full time and earning a master's degree. I put her financial affairs into order and took out a loan to pay the remaining nursing home bills she couldn't cover. When her decline worsened, I was the one to sign her DNR and organize her celebration of life. She passed in 2012, and I finally finished paying off this loan in 2021.

While at the height of my corporate career, I was in an abusive relationship but managed to get out.

I swallowed these challenges. I cannot remember ever having self-pity, only pure acceptance that this was my life, with the stoic wisdom that it was my job to work to make it better.

While incredibly difficult, I can honestly say that these challenges have never held me back. In fact, I could argue they have fueled my success and enabled me to build a life for my daughter that I always dreamed of. We live in a great neighborhood in Florida with excellent schools and opportunities available to her at every turn. She is as ambitious as I am but has the support that I never did. I can hardly wait to see what she will do with it.

In 2017, after spending more than twelve years working in Supply Chain and Retail Operations at Fortune 500 companies like Whirlpool and Office Depot/OfficeMax, I quit my job and founded Cannabis Business Growth. I've since worked with hundreds of incredible individuals in the cannabis space and have established a strategic partnership with The Cake House in California. I've found my purpose and deeply believe in the work I do.

Things have come full circle in a way. As my dad's friend told me, "It's the world's greatest irony to send you back to work in weed." My dad was an illegal drug dealer, which arguably created all the trauma in my life, and now I work in legal cannabis.

For all the challenges I have been presented with, my gift is the ability to navigate life in the face of adversity. It has fostered a hunger that propels me to break down any and all barriers that I face within or outside of my personal life. Given what I have seen with the impacts of the illicit market, addiction, and the huge potential for the plant to heal, it is only appropriate that I use what I have learned to advocate for cannabis.

For all intents and purposes, my family's circumstances—and my own life—would have been incredibly different if cannabis were readily accessible and legal. It is with that level of motivation and determination that I plan to continue to work toward *Breaking the Stigma*.

About Cannabis
Business Growth

C annabis Business Growth is the go-to cannabis business consultant for entrepreneurs working to establish and expand their footprints in the cannabis industry. We have consulted on more than three hundred projects across twenty-three states in five countries, winning more than seventy highly coveted cannabis licenses.

Whether you are a new or seasoned cannabis executive, you face many challenges in the cannabis industry—from the complicated regulatory framework, to the intricacies of running a retail store, to the strategic business planning required to navigate a constantly changing environment.

That's where we come in! Cannabis Business Growth's team of operational management professionals utilize decades of experience in both the traditional retail and cannabis spaces. With this background, we help cannabis startups and seasoned operators build businesses that are not only profitable and competitive, but will remain so for many years to come.

Cannabis Business Growth's extensive range of consulting services, with a focus on licensing and strategic business planning, will ensure your cannabis business gets the strong start and ongoing support it deserves.

We take a significant amount of pride in enabling our clients' success, because we believe in the plant and this industry. If you feel overwhelmed, are struggling to compete, or want to take your business to the next level, schedule a free thirty-minute consultation today to see how we can help.

For more information, visit https://www.cannabisbusinessgrowth.com and https://www.charlenaberry.com.

CPSIA information can be obtained
at www.ICGtesting.com
Printed in the USA
LVHW040048130322
713257LV00003B/200